My
Windows® 10

SECOND EDITION

Katherine Murray

800 East 96th Street,
Indianapolis, Indiana 46240 USA

My Windows® 10, Second Edition

Copyright © 2018 by Pearson Education, Inc.

ISBN-13: 978-0-7897-5980-1
ISBN-10: 0-7897-5980-2

Library of Congress Control Number: 2017962805
Printed in the United States of America
1 18

Trademarks

All terms mentioned in this book that are known to be trademarks or service marks have been appropriately capitalized. Que Publishing cannot attest to the accuracy of this information. Use of a term in this book should not be regarded as affecting the validity of any trademark or service mark.

Microsoft and/or its respective suppliers make no representations about the suitability of the information contained in the documents and related graphics published as part of the services for any purpose. All such documents and related graphics are provided "as is" without warranty of any kind. Microsoft and/or its respective suppliers hereby disclaim all warranties and conditions with regard to this information, including all warranties and conditions of merchantability, whether express, implied or statutory, fitness for a particular purpose, title and non-infringement. In no event shall Microsoft and/or its respective suppliers be liable for any special, indirect or consequential damages or any damages whatsoever resulting from loss of use, data or profits, whether in an action of contract, negligence or other tortious action, arising out of or in connection with the use or performance of information available from the services.

The documents and related graphics contained herein could include technical inaccuracies or typographical errors. Changes are periodically added to the information herein. Microsoft and/or its respective suppliers may make improvements and/or changes in the product(s) and/or the program(s) described herein at any time. Partial screenshots may be viewed in full within the software version specified.

Microsoft® and Windows® are registered trademarks of the Microsoft Corporation in the U.S.A. and other countries. Screenshots and icons are reprinted with permission from the Microsoft Corporation. This book is not sponsored or endorsed by or affiliated with the Microsoft Corporation.

Warning and Disclaimer

Every effort has been made to make this book as complete and as accurate as possible, but no warranty or fitness is implied. The information provided is on an "as is" basis. The author and the publisher shall have neither liability nor responsibility to any person or entity with respect to any loss or damages arising from the information contained in this book.

Special Sales

For information about buying this title in bulk quantities, or for special sales opportunities (which may include electronic versions; custom cover designs; and content particular to your business, training goals, marketing focus, or branding interests), please contact our corporate sales department at corpsales@pearsoned.com or (800) 382-3419.

For government sales inquiries, please contact governmentsales@pearsoned.com.

For questions about sales outside the U.S., please contact intlcs@pearson.com.

Editor-in-Chief
Greg Wiegand

Senior Acquisitions Editor
Laura Norman

Development Editor
Charlotte Kughen

Managing Editor
Sandra Schroeder

Editorial Services
The Wordsmithery LLC

Indexer
Cheryl Lenser

Proofreader
Gill Editorial Services

Technical Editor
Laura Acklen

Editorial Assistant
Cindy J. Teeters

Designer
Chuti Prasertsith

Compositor
Bronkella Publishing

Graphics
TJ Graham Art

Contents at a Glance

Table of Contents

4   Using Cortana: Your Personal Digital Assistant   85

7 Discovering, Using, and Sharing Favorite Apps   157

11 Bringing Out Your Inner Artist with Photos and Paint 3D   259

About the Author

After writing about technology for 35 years, Katherine Murray is still a computer geek. This is a fascinating time to be writing about technology. She has seen personal computing change from big, slow, cryptic desktop-hogging machines to small, sleek smart devices we easily can tap our way through. She has worked with every version of Microsoft Windows there's been, loving some versions (such as Windows 7) and loathing others. (Remember Windows Vista or, worse, Windows ME?) Katherine was part of the thumbs-up crowd when it came to Windows 8.1 but watched as Microsoft's vision tanked because users weren't quite ready for such a huge change in the way we work with our computers. Windows 10 Fall Creators Update represents the best of what Microsoft has learned about the balance of features, flashiness, and functionality, with even a little fun thrown in.

In addition to writing about technology, Katherine works as a hospice chaplain and pastors a Quaker church in Noblesville, Indiana.

Dedication

May the technology we use help us to create deeper, truer, kinder, and more creative connections with one another.

Acknowledgments

Thanks to all on the Que team for another great collaborative project. I appreciate all who were involved, from start to finish. Special thanks to Laura Norman for being so great to work with; to Charlotte Kughen for all her friendly help and great edits and questions along the way; and Laura Acklen, technical editor, for her good catches and funny notes.

We Want to Hear from You!

As the reader of this book, you are our most important critic and commentator. We value your opinion and want to know what we're doing right, what we could do better, what areas you'd like to see us publish in, and any other words of wisdom you're willing to pass our way.

We welcome your comments. You can email or write to let us know what you did or didn't like about this book—as well as what we can do to make our books better.

Please note that we cannot help you with technical problems related to the topic of this book.

When you write, please be sure to include this book's title and author as well as your name and email address. We will carefully review your comments and share them with the author and editors who worked on the book.

Email: feedback@quepublishing.com

Mail: Que Publishing
ATTN: Reader Feedback
800 East 96th Street
Indianapolis, IN 46240 USA

Reader Services

Visit our website and register this book at informit.com/register for convenient access to any updates, downloads, or errata that might be available for this book.

Introduction

It's taken a couple of generations (as least as far as software development goes), but with Windows 10 Creators Update, Microsoft is realizing some of the visionary features promised when the first blush of Windows 8 turned things upside-down. From the outset of this new approach to operating systems, developers envisioned a seamless computing experience that was consistent, smooth, and easy to use whether users were working on tablets, desktops, or phones. Developers also pictured an operating system that was built to help us spend our time on the things we're most interested in—social media, gaming, and creative efforts—without compromising anything in terms of productivity and security.

In the Creators Update of Windows 10, made available in September 2017, Microsoft delivers a slate of features designed to help users be more creative, take advantage of the latest technologies (such as virtual media and gaming enhancements), and streamline online tasks. Additionally, changes to the Cortana digital assistant mean users can access supportive services within apps; use touch to interact in new ways; and personalize the look, feel, and function of the operating system.

This book shows you all these new and enhanced features in Windows 10 Creators Update and provides all the coverage you need for essential tasks. Whether this is your first experience with the "new" Windows 10 or you've been following along since the first iteration of Windows 8, chances are that you'll be pleased (if not fascinated) by the tools and changes you'll find in these pages.

Versions of Windows 10

Windows 10 is available in two basic versions: Windows 10 Home and Windows 10 Pro. All the essential features are available in both versions; for example, the Start menu, live tiles, Cortana, Windows Ink, Microsoft Edge, game support, and numerous security features are part of the operating system no matter which version you use.

Beyond that, Windows 10 Pro offers additional features for those who will be using Windows 10 for professional tasks. Pro offers the additional security features of Windows Information Protection and Bitlocker and includes a number of business management tools, such as Mobile Device Management, group policy, Windows Store for Business, dynamic provisioning, shared PC configuration, and more. Additionally, Windows 10 Pro includes high-end networking and enterprise-level tools such as Domain Join, Remote Desktop, Enterprise Mode Internet Explorer, and Client Hyper-V.

Microsoft has recently introduced one more version of Windows 10, known as Windows 10 S. This version is a streamlined version of the operating system that focuses on security and efficiency without all the bells and whistles that can reduce system processing time.

Whichever version of Windows 10 you are currently using, the Windows 10 Creators Update will be installed automatically through Windows Updates.

Highlights of Windows 10 Creators Update

Windows 10, as the operating system of your desktop, tablet, and phone, is charged with many vital tasks that keep things running optimally and make sure you and your family—and the files and processes you use—are as safe as possible. Among the changes are new features that help boost your creativity, simplified processes that make picking up where you left off easier, enhanced security and privacy controls, and choices for personalization that enable you to tweak Windows 10 to work the way you do.

Specifically, you'll find these new and enhanced features in Windows 10 Creators Update:

- The Fluent Design is being used by Windows 10 app developers and is included in the Windows 10 interface as well. This gives your apps a consistent look and feel whether you're working on a desktop, tablet, or phone.

- The new Night Light feature dims the blue ratio of your screen after 9:00 p.m., which makes it easier on your eyes in darker environments. You can customize this feature to the schedule you prefer.

- Significant Cortana improvements bring the value of the digital assistant into apps you use every day. From within your favorite app (or the Microsoft Edge browser), you can ask for help and Cortana will spring into action. Cortana can also respond to commands to turn on or off your PC, change the volume, and play songs from Groove music.

- Creators Update also includes social improvements, such as the My People Hub, which enables you to keep up to three of your favorite contacts pinned to the hub on your taskbar so you can communicate easily with them throughout the day. There is also expanded support for shared experiences that enables you to share content, games, and sites across devices and with friends.

- Big enhancements in Microsoft Edge offer a way to set tabs aside (giving you more screen space), and you can preview tab thumbnails before you select them. Now you can now read PDFs and ePub files in the browser without needing an ereader app. To go along with the ebook feature, Windows Store includes thousands of ebooks you can download and read in Edge. The browser also includes a read-aloud feature so that you can listen to an audio book while you work on other things.

- Now Windows 10 has 3D support, thanks to Paint 3D and Remix 3D. Both creative tools enable you to create designs on the fly and extend your creation by showing it in different dimensions and environments. It's easier than you might think!

- Developers have focused on streamlining the behind-the-scenes processing in Windows 10 so that downloads happen faster, videos stream longer and without interruption, and the overall drain on the processor is lessened by significantly reducing the processing load. You'll notice that you spend less time waiting and more time being productive. This efficiency also extends to OneDrive, which now grabs the file you need "on demand," even though you can see all your OneDrive files in your File Explorer window. This reduces the amount of storage space you need on your computer or device, and the faster processing retrieves the file you need instantly, with no lag time.

- Gaming has gotten significant attention in Windows 10 Creators Update and has been given its own category in the Settings window. You can use the Game bar to control game flow, start live game broadcasting with Beam, and capture live audio and video of your gameplay.

- Windows 10 Creators Update is more secure than ever, with new ransomware protections, enhancements to Windows Defender Advanced Threat Protection that add specialized protection tools, and improvements to Defender's Antivirus tool.

What You'll Find in This Book

In this book, you'll discover what you need to know to accomplish all the basic tasks you want to do with Windows 10 Creators Update. The book focuses first on the features you're most likely to want to know up front; then it explores some of the more specialized tasks, such as working with File Explorer, navigating Microsoft Edge, and unboxing all the apps. The chapters unfold like this:

- Chapter 1, "Hello, Windows 10!" gets you started with the basics of Windows 10 and introduces you to all the key new features of the operating system. You learn how to use touch gestures, as well as the mouse and keyboard, to navigate with Windows 10 Creators Update. You also find out how to put Windows 10 to sleep, wake it up, and power down your computer, which you can now use Cortana and voice commands to do.

- Chapter 2, "Connecting and Managing Your Desktop and Devices," shows you Windows 10 functions in different domains—desktop, tablet, and phone. You find out how to add your phone to your Microsoft account so you can have a seamless experience no matter which device you may be using. You also find out about input improvements for the mouse, keyboard, and pen, and you learn about improvements in the process for adding new devices to Windows 10. You'll also find out how to set app notifications, make sure you have Internet access, learn about managing your PC's power, and find out how to refresh or reset your system.

- Chapter 3, "Accomplishing Windows 10 Essential Tasks," introduces you to the feel and functionality of the user interface in Windows 10. You take a tour of the desktop, as well as tablet mode, and learn how to set up Windows 10 to work the way you want it to. You find out how to tailor the Start experience so you have access to the apps and features you want most, and you see out how to manage the tools that are part of your daily life.

- Chapter 4, "Using Cortana: Your Personal Digital Assistant," introduces you to Cortana. Here you learn how to set up Cortana to work the way you do; teach Cortana to recognize your voice, and use voice commands to carry out basic tasks. You discover how Cortana can work alongside you, listening for commands as you create, research, produce, compile, or work with favorite apps, data, and sources.

- Chapter 5, "Personalizing Windows 10," covers all kinds of personaliza- tion features, beginning with customizations for the Lock screen, color schemes, profile picture, badges, notifications, and accessibility features. You find out how to set up the new Night Light feature, explore the new categories in Settings, and tweak the way apps work in the background. You also learn how to create multiple desktops in Windows 10 so that you can set up the apps and features for different people or places in your life.

- Chapter 6, "Securing Your Computer—for Yourself and Your Family," helps you ensure that your computer is as safe as possible by setting a password, customizing your login, creating user accounts, adding a PIN logon, setting location privacy, and telling Windows 10 how—or whether—you want apps to share your information. You're introduced to the new privacy tools so you can make nuanced choices about what you want to share online. You also find out about Windows Hello, which uses biometric login features to recognize faces, irises, and thumbprints. Additionally, in this chapter, you learn about setting up and using Family Safety features to safeguard your kids online.

- Chapter 7, "Discovering, Using, and Sharing Favorite Apps," introduces you to the redesigned Microsoft Store and shows you how to find, download, install, and update the apps that interest you. You find out how inking is now available in many popular apps and see how various apps work together to get you instant access to the information you need. This chapter also explains how to update apps and organize them on your system so that you easily can find the ones you need when you need them. This chapter also shows you the big new changes in the Microsoft Store—including thousands of ebook titles—and how to search for new apps you want to try.

- Chapter 8, "Working with Your Files in File Explorer and OneDrive," spotlights the tasks you need to know to organize your files and folders in Windows 10 Creators Update. Saving files to the cloud has become a big thing in recent years, and OneDrive is Microsoft's answer to in-the-cloud storage. In Windows 10, you can choose which folders you want to sync to the cloud so you can access the files you need easily, no matter which computer or device you may be using. You also find out about the new OneDrive on-demand file retrieval process, which opens only the file you need at a given time (freeing up storage space on your local computer or device). Along the way, you find out how to manage the changes in File Explorer and discover how easily you can copy, move, and share your files with others.

- Chapter 9, "Streamlined Surfing with Microsoft Edge," introduces the many new feature improvements in Microsoft's leading-edge browser. You're introduced to the new strategy for getting tabs out of the way (to give you more screen space), thumbnail previews for tabs, optimized processing for faster downloads and longer, smoother video streaming and browsing, and more. Also covered are the tools you use to read ebooks (PDFs or ePub files) in your Edge browser window, as well as the read-aloud feature that turns your ebook into an audio book. With Microsoft Edge, you can annotate web pages and share them easily with friends in your social media circles. You can use Edge's reading mode to clearly view the content on the pages that interest you (skipping the ads and formatting that are distracting).

- Chapter 10, "Staying in Touch (and in Sync) with Windows 10," walks you through the dramatic makeover of the Mail app and helps you set up the People app and learn how to add contact information for friends and family. You'll also learn about the Calendar app and find out how to use Skype to stay in touch with those on your Contacts list. This chapter also introduces the new My People hub, which you can use to keep close those contacts whom you regularly communicate with throughout the day.

- Chapter 11, "Bringing Out Your Inner Artist with Photos and Paint 3D," introduces you to tools in the Windows Photos app and showcases the new Paint 3D app and the Remix 3D community. These fun and creative tools take artistry to a whole new level by enabling you to design, create, and place 3D designs into different landscapes and perspectives.

- Chapter 12, "Getting Your Groove on with Favorite Music and Movies," shows you the ins and outs of the Windows 10 popular music service. You learn how to find the artists and albums you like, download music, play it the way you like, create playlists, and more. The chapter also introduces the Groove Music Service, explains how to create custom radio stations, and shows you how to play your favorite songs—by voice command—from the Windows 10 Lock screen. In addition, this chapter also shows you how to find, save, and watch your favorite shows and movies using Windows 10.

- Chapter 13, "Entertainment for the Gamer in You," uncovers the exciting new features in gaming. After a focus on basics—finding the game you want to play, launching it, and managing game play settings—you learn about game broadcasting with Beam, working with the new Game bar, turning on game mode to optimize your experience, and even recording audio and video while you play.

- Chapter 14, "Caring for Your Computer and Updating Windows," gives you some basic pointers on how to regularly back up your files, update your copy of Windows, and use Windows 10 system tools to improve your computer's performance and clean up your hard drive. In Windows 10 Creators Update, you have more control over how and when Windows is updated; this chapter shows you how to make that call. You also learn about the updates to Windows Narrator (now with Braille support).

The chapters are organized so that you can jump in and read about whatever interests you most, or you can choose to go through the book sequentially. Along the way are tips, notes, and two kinds of sidebars: Go Further, which gives you additional information about getting more from the topic at hand, and It's Not All Good, which lists common pitfalls and trouble spots to watch out for.

Let's Begin

Because Windows 10 Creators Update is an upgrade, it is delivered to your Windows 10 computer or device as part of the automatic update cycle. If you're curious and want to speed things along, you can choose Settings, click Update & Security, and choose Windows Update. Click or tap the Check for Updates button, and Windows 10 searches to see whether any new updates are available for your system.

Which Version of Windows 10 Do I Have?

To find out which version of Windows 10 you're currently using, click or tap the Start button, click or tap Settings, choose System, and then click or tap About. Scroll down to the Windows Specification settings to see which edition of Windows 10 your computer is running, which version (1703 or later is the Creators Update), and which OS build.

After the update is finished (it takes only a few minutes), you're prompted to restart your computer, and the update wraps up a few final details. Then, when you see the colorful image of the Windows 10 Lock screen, the process is complete. That's where you begin exploring Windows 10 Creators Update.

The Start menu gives
you access to all your
favorite apps.

Tablet mode displays
the app tiles full
screen.

In this chapter, you learn how to get started with Windows 10 and use touch, mouse, pen, and keyboard to perform tasks such as

→ Exploring Windows 10 Creators Update
→ Getting around with the mouse, keyboard, and pen
→ Using touch in Windows 10
→ Getting help in Windows 10
→ Shutting down or putting Windows 10 to sleep

Hello, Windows 10!

If you've been one of those Windows 7 hold-outs (and you're not alone!), waiting to try the latest version of Microsoft's Windows operating system until it seemed to stabilize and the bugs appeared to be worked out, now's your chance. Windows 10 is all that the developers of Windows 8 were hoping for when they first told us about all the great flexibility, the features that enable us to focus on what we love best, and the time-saving and click-reducing procedures that we could accomplish with a flick of the finger.

Windows 10 Creators Update, the latest version of Microsoft's innovative approach to the popular Windows operating system, offers new features designed to help you be more creative, stay safer (with new privacy tools and enhanced security features), and have more fun—with better browsing, expanded game support, 3D design tools, enhanced music and media tools, and more.

This chapter introduces you to Windows 10 and spotlights some of the new features you'll work with as you use apps, save files, share data, and enjoy media and games. This chapter also shows you how to get help when you need it, put your computer to sleep (no singing required), and power down the system completely, when you're ready to do that.

Exploring Windows 10 Creators Update

The latest version of Windows 10 will download and be installed to your computer automatically, so there's nothing you really need to do to get it.

The Windows Update utility restarts your computer after installation is complete. When your computer restarts, Windows 10 quickly appears on your screen, and it might walk you through a series of Express Setup questions (which help the operating system get you connected to the Internet, set your sharing preferences, and set up some surfing security features in Microsoft Edge). One of those questions asks you how you want to use your OneDrive account, which is the app that stores your files in the cloud. You can follow along with the onscreen prompts to set things up to your liking. After you finish answering all the necessary questions, Windows 10 lets you know that you are ready to begin, and the Windows 10 Lock screen appears.

Logging In to Windows 10

As the operating system for your computer, Windows 10 tells your hardware how to interact with the apps you use to communicate with others, work on files, and enjoy media. That means that when you press the Power button to start your computer or device, Windows 10 launches and begins doing its work. The following are the simple steps for starting your computer and logging in:

1. Press the Power button on your PC or device. After the system boots, your Windows 10 Lock screen appears, showing a beautiful landscape.

2. Click the screen (or swipe up if you have a touch-capable computer) or press any key to display the login page.

3. Enter your password and either press Enter or click the Submit arrow (not shown). Windows 10 logs you in.

Additional Sign-in Choices

Windows 10 offers other ways you can sign in if you like, although all you see on the login page is the Microsoft account you used when you first set up Windows 10. You can create a four-digit PIN for logging in; set up a feature called Windows Hello to enable face, fingerprint, or iris recognition; or create a picture password. You find out how to set up all these sign-in choices in Chapter 6, "Securing Your Computer—for Yourself and Your Family."

What Is a Microsoft Account?

During installation, Windows 10 asks you to log in to a Microsoft account, which is an email address and password that enables you to log in to all kinds of Microsoft services—such as OneDrive, Outlook.com, Skype, Xbox, and more—using a single login. When you log in to your Windows 10 computer or device using your Microsoft account, your preferences, such as screen backgrounds, app tile preferences, and even your browser favorites, are synced across all the devices you access using your Microsoft account.

Touring the Windows 10 Desktop

The screen you see when you first log in to Windows 10 depends on the type of computer you're using. If you're using a desktop PC, you see the Windows 10 desktop, with a large Recycle Bin in the upper-left corner of the screen and a set of tools (beginning with the Start button on the left) across the bottom of the screen.

The Start button displays the Start menu, which gives you access to all the apps on your computer or device (complete with live tiles). Just to the right of the Start button, you see a search box that reads Type Here to Search. This is also where you'll find Cortana lurking, waiting to act on your voice commands. You learn about the Start menu and discover how to set up Cortana in Chapter 3, "Accomplishing Windows 10 Essential Tasks."

In the middle of the taskbar, you see a few tools "pinned," which means they always stay visible as icons on the taskbar so you can find and use them easily. On the far right of the taskbar, you see the new My People hub icon, a set of icons giving you the status of various settings on your computer. (For example, the icons shown here represent network settings, volume, One-Drive, and Windows Ink Workspace.) To the right of the date and time, you see the Notifications tool, which lets you know when there are actions you need to take for Windows 10 or various apps on your system and shows you the number of notifications that have arrived since you last checked.

Recycle bin   **Windows 10 desktop**

Start button — Search box (and Cortana) — Taskbar pinned icons — My People hub — System icons — Notifications

Personalizing Your Start Experience

Windows 10 enables you to change the Start experience so it works in the way you're most comfortable with. By default, the Start menu appears when you click or tap the Start button in the lower-left corner of the screen. You can customize the options that appear in the lower portion of the menu so that the apps you use most often are within easiest reach. If you prefer, you can also have Windows 10 start up with the Start screen in full-screen tablet mode. See Chapter 3 to learn how to personalize your start experience.

Getting Started with Windows 10

As you begin exploring the new operating system, what are some of the first things you're likely to want to try? This section covers some of the big features in Windows 10, which are described in more detail throughout this book. (I've provided the chapter locations so you know where to go for more information.)

**Live tiles continually show
updated information.**

- **Use the Windows 10 Start menu**—The Start menu serves as a central point, giving you lots of information about friends, colleagues, weather, email, and more. You can see at a glance the number of email messages you have, what your day's appointments look like, and what the news headlines are. You can also start your favorite apps, play media, change system settings, and even customize the look of Windows, all from this one screen. You find out how to tweak the look of the Start menu in Chapter 5, "Personalizing Windows 10."

- **Launch and work with apps**—The colorful tiles on the Windows 10 Start menu represent apps, or programs, you can launch with a simple click or tap. Some apps display "live" information and update on the Start menu, and others don't. You learn how to work with, organize, and get new apps in Chapter 7, "Discovering, Using, and Sharing Favorite Apps."

Arrange Apps Your Way

You can easily group, name, and work with clusters of apps so that you can find what you need quickly. You learn how to do this in Chapter 7.

- **Browse the Web with Microsoft Edge**—Microsoft Edge is Microsoft's web browser, which replaced Internet Explorer 11. (You can still download and install IE if you want.) Edge integrates easily with the Cortana digital assistant and is able to display personalized search information, as well as support handwritten notes on web pages. Edge also includes a reading mode that suppresses the display of formatting and advertisements to make reading web content easier. You find out more about using Microsoft Edge in Chapter 9, "Streamlined Surfing with Microsoft Edge."

- **Stay in contact with friends and family**—The new My People hub can pull together your closest contacts so they are available throughout the day for quick communication.

The My People hub keeps your
favorite contacts close.

- **Find new favorites in the Microsoft Store**—The Microsoft Store is greatly improved in Windows 10, including thousands of new apps and even more ebooks, ready for downloading. In the Microsoft Store, you can find apps of all kinds, free and otherwise. You find out more about browsing and shopping in the Microsoft Store in Chapter 7.

- **Listen to your favorite music or watch a show**—The improved Groove Music app, and the Groove Music Service, make it easy for you to play your favorite songs in any combination you like. You can create your own radio stations, playlists, and more. And the Movies & TV app gives you a way to watch your favorite movies and shows—binge-watching at its best.

- **Go for a little gaming**—More and more, in our hectic and stressful world, a game gives us a way to quiet our minds and have some fun. Windows 10 has a slate of games and new gaming features that make gameplay easier and more seamless than ever. You can play solo or broadcast your game and play along with friends.

**New Windows 10 Game
bar in Xbox app**

- **Use Windows 10 your way**—In Windows 10, you can see all the apps you have installed by scrolling through them in the Start menu. This is similar to the All Programs functionality in the Windows 7 Start menu. All the apps are all organized in alphabetical order. You can scroll through the list by dragging the scrollbar and then clicking the app you want to open.

Move to an App Quickly

If you're scrolling through the apps list and want to move quickly to another part of the alphabet, click or tap one of the alphabetical letters to display a grid of letters, and then choose the beginning letter of the apps you want to see. This action takes you directly to that letter in the list—no scrolling required.

Click or tap a   **Scroll through**
letter to display   **the list to review**
a letter grid.   **your apps.**

Getting Around with the Mouse, Keyboard, and Pen

If you're using a desktop computer or a docked tablet with a mouse and keyboard, chances are that mouse techniques are old hat and you know your way around a keyboard. What you might *not* know, however, are some of the particulars of Windows 10. That's what this section is all about.

Using the Mouse

The mouse can get you anywhere you want to go in Windows 10, and the mouse has been our trusted naviga- tional companion for decades now. Even tablet users often attach a "real" mouse and keyboard when they sit down to do serious work on their computers.

In Windows 10, you use the mouse for all the common tasks: starting apps, finding and opening files, choosing program settings, working with media, playing games, and so on. Here are some of the common techniques you might already be using:

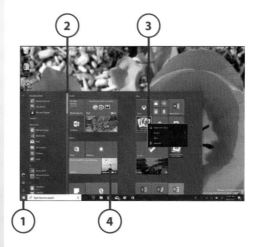

1. Click the Start button to display the Start menu.

2. Use the vertical scrollbar to scroll through available apps.

3. Right-click the app tile in the Start menu to display a context menu for that app. From there, you can click the option you want to use.

4. Click an app name or an app tile to launch the app.

Selecting Multiple Items

In File Explorer, you can use the mouse and keyboard together to select mul- tiple items at once. If you want to choose several files in a folder, for example, you can click the first item and then press and hold the Shift key and click the last item you want to select. All items between the two clicked items are selected.

If you want to select multiple items that aren't next to each other, click the first item and then press and hold the Ctrl key; then click all the other items you want to include.

Mouse Shortcuts for Navigating Windows 10

To do this:	Do this:
Unlock your Lock screen.	Click any mouse button.
Scroll through the Start menu.	Click All Apps and drag the vertical scrollbar on the right side of the left column in the menu.
Show "power user menu."	Right-click the Windows 10 Start button.
Display app context menu on the Start menu.	Right-click the app tile.
Change or personalize settings for your Windows 10 desktop.	Right-click anywhere on the desktop and click Display Settings or Personalize.
Display Task view.	Click the Task View icon in the Quick Launch area of the desktop taskbar.

Getting to the Menu

If you know what you're looking for in Windows 10 and want to get right to it, you might enjoy using what some people are calling the "power user menu" that appears when you right-click the Start button. You can also display it by pressing Windows+X on your computer keyboard or your tablet's onscreen keyboard.

The list of features includes many of those you might have seen in the Windows Control Panel previously: Apps and Features, Mobility Center, Power Options, Device Manager, Run, and more. Click the feature you want to use, or, to hide the feature list, tap or click anywhere outside the list.

Right-click the Start button to display the power user menu.

Using the (Real) Keyboard

For some of the things you'll do in Windows 10, you'll want a real, live keyboard. Sure, you can type a quick memo or answer an email message on your tablet using the onscreen keyboard. But when you need to write a 10-page report for a departmental meeting or you have lots of work to do storyboarding the next team presentation, chances are you'll want to use a traditional keyboard with real keys to press.

In addition to using touch and the mouse, you can use your keyboard for navigating in Windows 10. When you use your keyboard to navigate the Start menu, move among apps, and manage windows, you use special keys, shortcut key combinations, and function keys.

- The Windows key, commonly located on the lowest row of your keyboard on the left side between the Ctrl and Alt keys, takes you back to the Start menu no matter where you are in Windows 10.

- You can use the Page Up and Page Down keys as well as the arrow keys to move among apps if you're on the Windows 10 Start screen.

- You can use the Tab key to move from option to option.

- You can press key combinations (such as Ctrl and the letter assigned to a specific menu option) to perform operations.

Keyboard Shortcuts for Navigating Windows 10

To do this:	Do this:
Unlock your Lock screen.	Press any key on the keyboard.
Display the Settings app.	Press Windows+I.
Open the Search window.	Press Windows+Q.
Display the Start menu.	Press the Windows key.
Lock Windows 10.	Press Windows+L.
Display power user commands.	Press Windows+X.
Display Task view.	Press Windows+Tab.
Cycle through open apps.	Press Alt+Tab.
Create a new desktop in Windows 10.	Press Windows+Ctrl+D.
Switch between desktops in Windows 10.	Press Windows+Ctrl+left arrow (or right arrow).
Close the current desktop.	Press Windows+Ctrl+F4.
Minimizes an app.	Press Windows+Down.
Maximizes an app.	Press Windows+Up.
Open Control Panel.	Press Windows+X+P.

A Keyboard Is a Keyboard Is a Keyboard…Right?

Depending on the type of computer you are using, you might notice some differences in the ways certain keys appear on your keyboard. The keyboard mentioned here is a "basic" keyboard layout. Your keyboard might or might not have a separate numeric keypad, function keys across the top, and a set of cursor-control keys that are separate from the alphanumeric keys. Additionally, you may notice that your Delete key or Backspace key is in a slightly different place than on other keyboards you see. Take the time to learn where to find the common keys on your Windows 10 keyboard; when you know the lay of the land, finding the right key at the right time will be second nature.

Using a Touch Keyboard

If you're using a touch device, you might not plan to type whole books on your onscreen keyboard, but it's nice to know you can use it when you need it. Windows 10 helps you with your typing by adding auto-text that offers word suggestions as you type; it also extends the function of the keyboard by including child keys that appear on the keyboard when you press and hold a specific key. This gives you easy access to the keys you need.

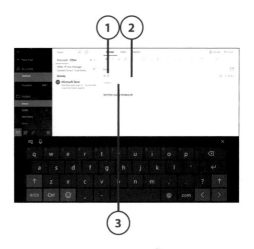

Begin by launching an app that requires you to type something on your tablet. For example, you might open the Mail app and start a new message. Then follow these steps to display and work with the Windows 10 touch keyboard:

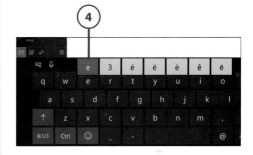

1. Tap in the To area. The full keyboard appears along the bottom half of your screen.

2. Type the email address of the person to whom you want to send the message.

3. Tap in the subject line and use the keyboard to enter the topic of the message.

4. Press and hold a key to display child keys for some keys—for example, vowels that can have different accents, such as the vowels *a*, *e*, *i*, *o*, and *u*, and punctuation characters such as the period (.), apostrophe ('), and question mark (?).

Choosing a Keyboard

Windows 10 gives several types of touch keyboards to use, and you can easily change the keyboard as you're using it. The standard keyboard offers all the basic keys you need and gives you the option of switching to show numbers and punctuation; the thumbs keyboard groups the keyboard on both sides of the screen so you can type with your thumbs on a tablet or other touch device. The extended keyboard displays all alphanumeric keys, as well as punctuation keys, Alt, Ctrl, and more.

Child Keys Aren't Available on the Extended Keyboard

If you want to use child keys on your onscreen keyboard, choose the standard or thumbs keyboard, because child keys don't appear when you're using the extended keyboard.

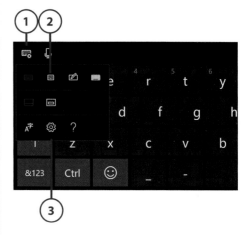

1. If you want to change the type of keyboard displayed, tap the keyboard button in the upper-left corner of the keyboard.

2. A set of four choices appears. You can choose from the onscreen touch keyboard, a thumbs keyboard, a drawing tablet, or the standard keyboard. Tap the keyboard you want to use.

3. You can also change your keyboard settings by tapping Language Preferences, Typing Settings, or Keyboard Tips.

Using Speech with the Keyboard

In Windows 10 Creators Update, you also can dictate your content right into the app open on the screen. In the upper-left corner of the touch keyboard, the Microphone icon is the tool you need.

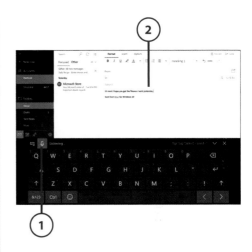

1. With the touch keyboard displayed, tap the Microphone icon. A red Listening indicator appears.

2. Speak the text you want to add. It appears at the cursor position.

3. When you're finished entering text, say "Stop dictating," and the red indicator disappears.

Using a Pen with the Keyboard

Are you getting the feeling that the keyboard isn't just for typing anymore? Developers know you're likely to use Windows 10 on a variety of computers and devices (at least, they *hope* you will), so having more than one input option is essential. If you find it easier to handwrite notes or other content, you can use your pen to input information in common Windows 10 apps.

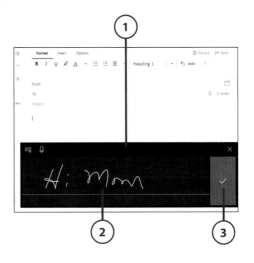

1. Choose the writing pad in the keyboard options. The writing pad appears in place of the traditional keyboard.

2. Use your pen to write the content you want to add. Windows 10 converts your handwriting to typed text.

3. When you're finished, tap the check mark.

Repositioning the Keyboard

We all have our preferences for the way we like to type. Some prefer larger keys that click; others have gotten used to texting on smartphones and spell at lightning speed on the smallest of keys. Windows 10 gives you a new option for tweaking your touch keyboard; now you can reposition the keyboard and move it to any point onscreen that makes sense to you.

You might want to move the keyboard, for example, when you're adding data to a worksheet with information you want to show at the bottom of your display; or perhaps you're trying to keep a chart and a table in view while you add a note about the chart's contents.

Using your finger or pen, drag the top of the touch keyboard in the direction you desire. Release the keyboard in the new location.

Displaying the Emoji Keyboard

As part of the touch keyboard, Windows 10 includes a new emoji keyboard that enables you to add fun and flair to some of your apps. Note that not all apps are able to make use of the new keyboard, but for the ones that can, you can to choose from a sweeping range of emojis in many colorful categories, as well as 25 different languages.

1. On the touch keyboard, tap the smiley face button. The emoji keyboard appears.

2. Click the category of emoji you want to see.

3. Choose the emoji you want to insert into your app.

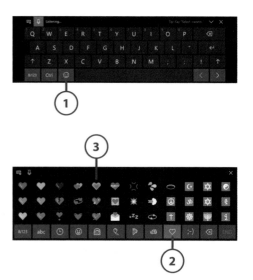

>>>Go Further

SAY WHAT?!

Windows 10 includes the Narrator accessibility feature, which reads the screen so people with visual challenges can interact successfully with Windows 10. Narrator has been around for several incarnations of Windows and offers natural-sounding voices. (You can choose from three PC voices—two female voices and one male voice.) You can also control the speed at which Windows narrates your experience, which can be helpful if you're just learning how to use voice to navigate the operating system.

You can turn on Narrator as soon as you open the Lock screen, before you even log in to your computer. Simply tap the Ease of Use button in the lower-right corner of the login screen to begin the narration. You can also turn on Narrator by pressing and holding the Windows key and tapping the Volume Up button on your keyboard.

Microsoft Edge includes Narrator support as well, so users can listen to web content, understand links, and make choices about commands on web pages.

Using Touch in Windows 10

Because Windows 10 is designed to go with you no matter what device you might be using—computer, tablet, smartphone—the operating system needs to be able to interact with users in a variety of ways. One of the visions behind the redesign of Windows years ago was the intention to make the software touch-friendly, so people could seamlessly do what they wanted to do across formats.

If you have a smartphone, you already know about touch. You tap the surface of your phone to dial a friend's number, you swipe through photos, you pinch a web page to make the print larger (so you can read it on that small screen). Windows even includes a "hands-free mode" for apps that support it.

If you use Windows 10 on a tablet or touch-enabled screen, you'll notice you can interact with Windows much the way you use your smartphone. However, for good measure (and for those readers who don't go for the smartphones), this section introduces the gestures you're likely to use most often in Windows 10 and takes a look at the new gestures added into this release.

Using Single Tap

You tap the screen to launch an app on the Windows 10 Start screen, select a setting, or choose an item to display.

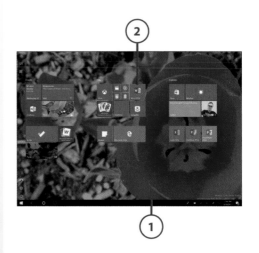

1. Launch Windows 10 on your tablet, and the Start screen appears.

2. Tap once quickly in the center of the tile or icon. If you tapped an application on the Start screen, the program opens; if you tapped a setting or an option, the item is selected or displays additional choices, if applicable.

Tap and Hold

In a mouse world, you can display a context menu of options for different objects (files, folders, and apps) by right-clicking them. In the touch world, the equivalent of that right-click is a tap-and-hold gesture:

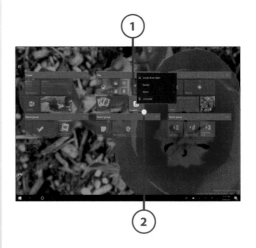

1. Tap and hold an app tile. Two circles appear in the upper- and lower-right corners of the tile.

2. Tap the lower circle displaying the three dots. This displays the context menu. Tap the option you want to apply.

Swiping Right

The swipe-right gesture enables you to swipe open apps in from the left edge of the screen and display them in Task view. If you don't have any additional apps open, there will be no app to swipe in. You can also use the swipe-left gesture when you're using Microsoft Edge to browse the Web.

1. Display the Windows 10 Start screen on your tablet.

2. Touch a point toward the left side of the Start screen and drag to the right. Your open apps appear as thumbnails in the center of the display.

More About Task View
You learn more about working with apps in Task view in Chapter 3.

Swiping Left

You use the swipe-left gesture to display the Notifications panel in Windows 10.

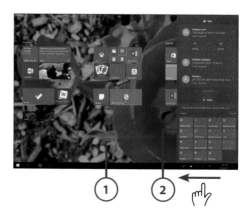

1. Display the Windows Start screen on your tablet.

2. Touch the screen close to the right edge and drag in to the left. The Notifications panel scrolls in from the right.

Swiping Up and Down

You'll use the swiping up and down gesture when you want to work with different apps. You also swipe up and down when you are scrolling through apps on the Windows 10 Start screen.

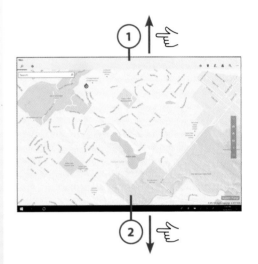

1. To swipe up on the screen, press and hold and drag the display upward.

2. To swipe down, touch the screen and swipe down toward the bottom of the screen.

Swipe Down to Close

One of the big criticisms of the early release of Windows 8 was that initially Windows developers didn't provide a way to close apps because Windows 8 actually suspended apps not in use (which meant that technically you didn't need to close them). In Windows 10, developers added a Close box in the expected place (the upper-right corner of the app window) so that when you want to close the app, you can tap or click the Close box. To display the title bar (which includes the Close box), swipe down from the top of the screen.

Using Pinch Zoom

The pinch-zoom gesture enables you to enlarge and reduce the size of the content on the screen. When you pinch your fingers together, the content reduces in size. When you want to enlarge an area of the screen, you use your fingers to expand the area, and the screen magnifies along with your gesture.

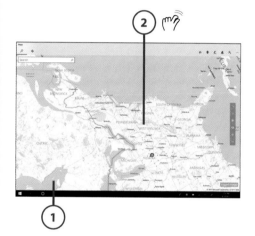

1. Display the app you want to use.

2. Reduce the size of the content displayed by placing your thumb and forefinger on the screen and "pinching" the area together.

3. Enlarge an area of the screen by placing your thumb and forefinger together on the screen and expanding the distance between them (not shown).

Semantic Zoom

You might see this feature referred to as *semantic zoom*, so named because it enables you to magnify a specific region of the display without disturbing other parts of the screen. If the app you're using was designed for Windows 10, chances are that it supports the pinch-zoom gesture. That means you can use two fingers to change the size of the content displayed on the screen.

>>>Go Further
NEW GESTURES IN WINDOWS 10

Early on in the development of Windows 10, developers announced several new gestures that enable Windows 10 users to take better advantage of trackpad capabilities. The Mac OS has had similar gestures for some time, but Microsoft has come up with simplified versions. Note that not all trackpads will have the capacity to allow these gestures, but if your system does, you might find these handy:

- **Three-finger swipe down**—You can hide open windows and display the Windows desktop by swiping down with three fingers on the trackpad.

- **Three-finger swipe up**—If you have recently hidden your windows (as described in the previous gesture), you can return your windows to the screen by using three fingers to swipe up on the trackpad. If you have not previously hidden your windows, swiping up in this way displays Task view.

- **Three-finger swipe right and left**—You can page through open apps (similar to using Alt+Tab to move through open apps) by swiping in from the right or left using three fingers on your trackpad.

Getting Help in Windows 10

No matter where you are in Windows 10 or what you're doing, help is always within reach. Depending on the type of help you need—maybe just a quick refresher on the task you haven't done in a while—the best place to begin is the Search box on your Windows 10 taskbar.

1. Display the Start screen by clicking or tapping the Windows button.

2. Enter a word or phrase that represents what you need help with.

3. Click or tap a right arrow to display help options for the topic
you choose.

4. Click a category to determine
what kind of answer you'd like.

5. Choose to see a larger list of
search results.

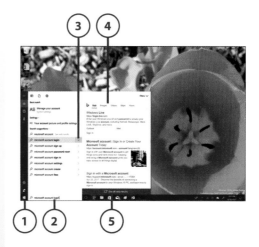

Using the Tips App

The Tips app is another helpful tool
in Windows 10 that is designed to
give you the answers you need as
you work with your operating system
and apps. You'll find the app under
T in the All Apps list in your Start
menu, or you can just type **Tips** in
the Search box and Windows 10 finds
it for you.

1. Click or tap the Windows button
to display the Start menu.

2. Scroll to the apps beginning with
the letter *T*.

3. Click or tap Tips.

4. Click the type of tips you'd like to see.

5. Click or tap a tile to find out more about the topic.

Don't See What You're Looking for?

If you scroll through tips but aren't seeing anything particularly helpful, click in the Search box at the top of the left column and type a word or phrase describing what you'd like to know more about. You might enter, for example, *how to set a reminder or adding a new user account.*

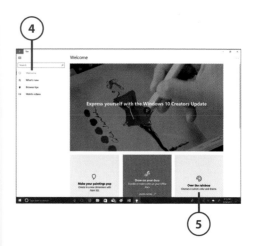

Shutting Down or Putting Windows 10 to Sleep

Another common task you might want to do regularly with Windows 10 is turn off your computer. In previous versions of Windows, Microsoft hid the Power tool from view, but in Windows 10 it has been returned to a prominent place. If you're using the mouse, you'll find the Power tool toward the bottom of the Start menu; if you're using tablet mode, the Power tool appears in the lower-left corner of the screen.

Sleep Tight

With Windows 10 Creators Update, you can rely on Cortana to do the heavy lifting for you. If your computer is on and idle, you can simply say, "Hey, Cortana!" and the personal digital assistant awakens. You can then tell Cortana to "shut down" or "sleep," and the computer does what you request. You find out how to set up Cortana to carry out this task for you in Chapter 4, "Using Cortana: Your Personal Digital Assistant."

Goodnight, Windows 10

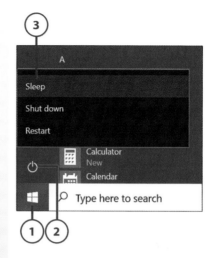

When you're going to be away from your computer for a period of time, but you aren't ready to turn everything off for the day, you can put your computer in Sleep mode to conserve energy and protect your files and programs while you're away.

1. Click or tap the Start button to display the Start menu.

2. Click or tap the Power tool toward the bottom of the menu. A list of options appears: Sleep, Shut Down, Restart.

3. Click or tap Sleep.

Shutting Down Windows 10

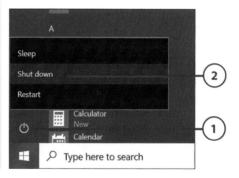

Use the Shut Down tool when you're ready to turn your computer completely off.

1. On the Start menu, click or tap Power.

2. Click or tap Shut Down. If you have any open, unsaved files, Windows 10 prompts you to save them before shutting down.

Wake Up, Little Fella

One of the great things about Sleep mode is that it's designed to help your computer spring back to life quickly as soon as you're ready. So even though it's a little distressing to see everything fade to black so quickly after you tap Sleep, you'll be pleased to know a simple tap of the Power button on your PC brings everything back to full wakefulness almost instantly.

Starting Over

You have one more option when you tap or click Power. If you want to restart your computer, you can tap or click Restart; Windows 10 powers down and then starts again. You might be asked to restart your computer after you install an app or make a system setting change.

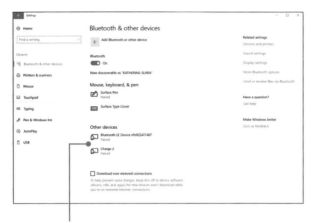

Windows 10 discovers and adds your devices automatically.

You can access Settings from the Start menu.

This chapter helps you get your computer and devices ready to use with the following tasks:

→ Adding devices in Windows 10
→ Connecting to wireless networks
→ Linking your phone to Windows 10
→ Managing your PC power
→ Resetting Windows 10

Connecting and Managing Your Desktop and Devices

One of the biggest stories about Windows 10 has been a long time coming. The early promise was that the operating system would provide a consistent look and feel across all your computers and devices. The Windows 10 Creators Update takes a big step in that direction, creating a sense of consistency whether you are using a computer, a tablet, or a phone.

Windows 10 adjusts easily and instantly when you undock your tablet and go. You might have been using Windows 10 as a desktop computer, but when you undock the tablet and hit the road, Windows 10 automatically goes into tablet mode, offering the same functionality presented in the best way for the device you're taking along.

The fact that the software automatically takes care of this for you means that you'll be able to focus on the tasks at hand: calling up a presentation, navigating your notes, and sharing important data with clients or colleagues as needed. The screens in each format have differences but are very similar to each other, giving you access to the same basic tools in different screen configurations built for each device.

Windows 10 helps you easily prepare your PC and get things up and running. Much of what happens behind the scenes doesn't need your involvement at all. For example, if you're using Windows 10 on a computer with a keyboard and a mouse, Windows 10 recognizes that and provides you with setup options related to that usage scenario. If you're using Windows 10 on a touch device, it enables touch features so that the touch keyboard and other touch features are within reach in all the tasks and tools you use in Windows 10.

When you log in with your Microsoft Account, your preferences for theme, background, user preferences, and even browser favorites are saved so that you have a fairly consistent experience across multiple devices. What's more, with the new Link Phone category in Settings, you can link your phone to Windows 10 no matter which type of phone—Windows Phone, Android, or iPhone—you are using. That way, you can easily access and share your favorite music, photos, videos, and more—no matter where they reside.

You can also set up other devices to work with your Windows 10 computer. This might include a tablet (one or many), your Xbox, or something else. Windows 10 makes it easy to add devices and get them working smoothly with the operating system. This chapter helps you explore those steps and get things ready to run with Windows 10.

Before You Proceed

This chapter focuses on some simple setup tasks for your Windows PC that I think you'll want to get into right away. However, if you're having a difficult time navigating your way around, consider jumping ahead to Chapter 3, "Accomplishing Windows 10 Essential Tasks," and then come back when you're up to speed.

Adding Devices in Windows 10

Windows 10 includes an autodiscovery feature that scans for all devices connected to your PC or your network. When Windows 10 detects those devices, it then connects to those printers, TVs, Xbox systems, and more. This means Windows 10 might be able to find and install all your computer peripherals automatically, and you won't need to do anything at all! Wouldn't that be nice?

The first step involves using Settings to see which devices Windows 10 has already discovered and added to your system. You can then add a device if you have one that isn't included on the generated list or remove devices that were installed but that you are no longer using.

Viewing Installed Devices

You can take a look at the devices Windows 10 has found and installed automatically as part of your setup. And then you can add a device or remove devices that were added but that you no longer need. To display the list, follow these steps:

1. Click the Start button to display the Windows 10 Start menu. (You learn more about the Start button in Chapter 3.)

2. Choose Settings.

3. Select Devices in the top row of the Settings window.

4. Review the devices listed in the center of the window.

Adding a Device

If Windows 10 missed one of the devices you think should be on the device list, you can scan again to see whether the device is discoverable. Before you tap or click Add Bluetooth or Other Device, be sure the device is connected to your computer or your home network and turned on. After you select Add Bluetooth or Other Device, Windows 10 scans your computer and shows any found devices in a pop-up list. You can then select the item you want to add to the Devices list.

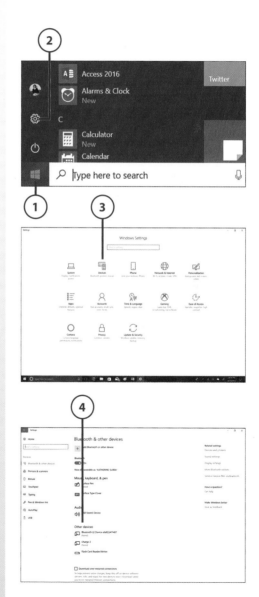

Connecting Unrecognized Devices

If you connect your device to Windows 10 and the operating system doesn't recognize the device you added, Windows 10 displays a message that you need to finish the setup in the Action Center. Click the link displayed in the message to go to the Action Center, and follow the steps to download and install the files needed to get your device running smoothly.

Removing a Device

You can remove a device you no longer need from the Devices list. Having extra devices in the Devices list doesn't do any harm, but if you want to keep the list short so you can easily find what you need, you might want to take any unnecessary items off the list.

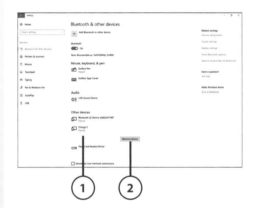

1. Click the device you want to remove from the list.

2. If you're sure you want to remove the device, click the Remove Device button. Windows 10 removes the item from the list.

Troubleshoot USB Connections

Typically you're able to plug in a device using your USB port, and Windows 10 takes it from there. On the off chance that something happens and the USB port isn't responding properly, Windows 10 notifies you. To view the setting or turn it off, display the Devices page of Settings, click USB, and uncheck the check box in the list that will stop connected devices.

>>>Go Further

TROUBLESHOOTING HARDWARE DEVICES

As computers have gotten easier to use, by and large they have become self-corrective. Most of the time, your printer, router, scanner, camera, and drawing tablet function the way they're supposed to. You plug them in to your Windows 10 PC, Windows finds the right drivers, and they're ready for you to use. But once in a while, devices have trouble. Your printer doesn't print anything. Your router is blinking, but you have no Internet connection. Windows doesn't seem to be recognizing your fitness tracker. When that happens, you can use one of the Windows 10 troubleshooting tools to help you discover and fix the problem.

To access the troubleshooter, click the Search box to the right of the Start button and type **troubleshoot**; this will bring up a list of results. Click Troubleshoot in the results list to return the Troubleshoot screen in the Update & Security category of Settings. Next, click Hardware and Devices in the list in the center and then click Run the Troubleshooter.

Windows 10 now attempts to diagnose your PC's problems. When a fix is found, click Apply This Fix to apply the fix or Skip This Fix to skip the current suggested fix and have Windows 10 continue troubleshooting. When the troubleshooter has finished, Windows 10 displays a list of problems it was unable to fix automatically. From here you can either click Explore Additional Options to see extra information or click Close to close the troubleshooter.

Connecting to Wireless Networks

In today's world, we're almost always connected. We go from the corporate network at work, to Bluetooth or mobile connectivity on the road, to Wi-Fi at the neighborhood coffee shop. Windows 10 makes the change right along with you, discovering networks in your area and giving you the capability to connect (if you have the password or network key, of course) by tapping the connection you want to make. You can easily switch among networks by using the Network & Internet tool in Settings.

Connecting to an Available Network

Now in Windows 10 you can connect to available wireless networks by using the Networks tool in the notifications area in the lower-right corner of your screen. You'll find the tool to the left of the Volume tool in the system tray (on the right side of the taskbar).

When you click or tap the Networks tool, Windows 10 displays a list of the wireless networks in your vicinity. You can then connect to the network of your choice by selecting it and entering a password if necessary.

1. Click the Networks tool in the notifications area on the right side of the status bar to display the list of available networks.

2. Click the network you want to connect to, and click Connect. If you want to disconnect from a network to which you're connected, tap or click the Disconnect button.

3. If you want Windows 10 to connect to the network automatically whenever it's present, click or tap the Connect Automatically check box.

Other Network Options

While you're working in the Network & Internet Settings window, you can also extend the network connections currently in place for your Windows 10 PC or device. You can scroll down to Change Your Network Settings and click HomeGroup to set up a network group where other computers and devices (including your Xbox 360 and Xbox One) can access files and media on your computer.

Linking Your Phone to Windows 10

To help you work seamlessly no matter which device you're using at the moment, Microsoft has included a new Phone category in Windows 10 settings that enables you to link your phone to Windows. This means you're able to share files among your devices and easily pick up where you left off when you're switching from laptop to phone to tablet and back again.

This is especially good news for you if you're an Android or iOS user because when you add the Microsoft Apps tool to your mobile device (Windows 10 will send you a link to that download when you link your phone in Settings), you're able to carry your work easily between devices.

Adding Your Phone to Windows 10

1. Click or tap the Start button to reveal the Start menu.

2. Click or tap Settings.

3. Click or tap Phone.

4. Click or tap Add a Phone. A dialog box opens, asking you to enter your mobile phone number.

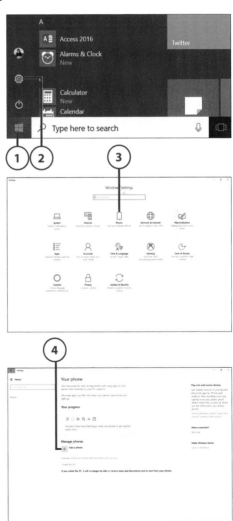

5. Type the mobile number of the phone you want to add.

6. Click or tap Send. Windows 10 sends a text message to your Android or iOS phone that includes a link you can follow to download the Microsoft Apps tool.

7. Click Close to finish adding the phone.

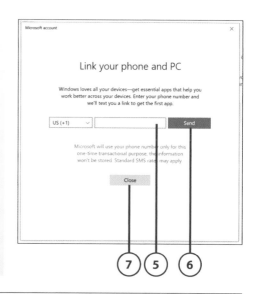

Hello, Windows Phone

If you are using a Windows Phone, Windows 10 Creators Update recognizes it automatically if you have logged into the phone using your Microsoft Account.

You can see whether your phone is linked to your Microsoft account by choosing Phone in the Settings window and then clicking Manage All Devices Linked to Your Microsoft Account. Windows 10 shows you all the devices currently linked to your account and gives you the means to change them if you'd like. You also automatically find your Windows Phone listed under This PC in File Explorer when the phone is connected to your computer. That means you can easily access files—such as photos, music, and more—stored on your phone, in the same way you would access any flash drive or other device connected to your system.

Where's the Windows Phone App?

Now, because Windows 10 Creators Update automatically integrates support for Windows Phone, you no longer need a special app to manage the connection for you. So, the Windows Phone App went away with this latest update because it's no longer needed.

Managing Your PC Power

Thankfully, as computer makers continue to improve the hardware they offer, our computers and devices are becoming more energy efficient. This is good not only for our bank accounts, but also for our planet. We want the batteries in our laptops, tablets, and smartphones to last as long as possible. The more power we conserve, the more efficient our devices become, the longer our power lasts—and that's a good thing.

One thing we've learned about "green tech" is that small changes can make a big difference. Changing the brightness of your screen or turning off Wi-Fi and roaming when possible can save a lot of behind-the-scenes processing. Even reducing energy consumption on your home desktop PC can have tangible benefits, such as reducing your electric bill. Those simple techniques, added to steps such as thinking through what happens when you close your laptop cover, can add up to smarter energy use for us all.

Windows 10 is the most energy-efficient version of Windows yet, with careful attention paid to apps that are in the foreground. Apps that cycle to the background and go into suspended mode have no impact on power usage at all. And because Windows 10 boots so efficiently, you won't experience any lag time while you wait for an app to load. That's a big change from the days you could push the power button and then go to the kitchen to get a cup of coffee while waiting for your computer to boot.

Turning On the Battery Saver

The Battery Saver app in Windows 10 enables you to control how your computer or device uses power. By default, Windows 10 turns on Battery Saver mode when power gets to 20%; but you can change that if you want. You can also adjust the way your computer or device is using power on the fly—that's something new with Windows 10 Creators Update.

You can check your power status easily by clicking the Power tool in the system tray on the right side of the taskbar. If your computer is currently plugged in, the status shows 100% power. If your computer is using the battery, the status of the battery, the estimated amount of time remaining, and an active link to Battery Settings appear.

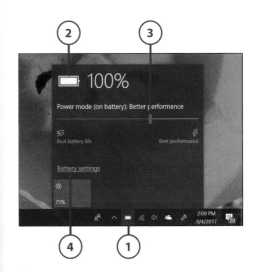

1. Click the Power tool.

2. Review the battery status.

3. Adjust the slider to reflect whether you would prefer to save battery or have better performance.

4. Click Battery Settings to see additional options.

5. Drag the Battery Saver slider if you want to change the percentage at which the battery saver goes into effect.

6. Enable the Battery Saver Status Until Next Charge setting if you want to put your computer into Battery Saver mode until the next time it is charged.

7. Uncheck the Lower Screen Brightness While in Battery Saver check box if you want to turn off the Battery Saver setting that displays a lower percentage of screen brightness. (This setting is enabled by default.)

8. Click Battery Usage by App to review how your various apps are making use of your battery power.

9. Review how much battery life your apps are using.

10. Choose whether you want to see all apps or apps that have been running within a period of time you specify.

11. Click an app that you want to change.

12. Click to remove the check in the Let Windows Decide When This App Can Run in the Background check box if you want to manually control the use of battery power.

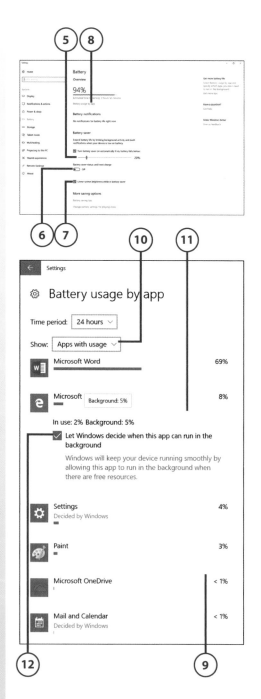

Changing Your Power Settings

You can also manage the way your computer uses power by choosing the power settings you want Windows 10 to use. The Balanced power plan balances usage with performance, and you can change that balance as needed while you work. Making changes is as simple as pointing and clicking.

1. Click in the Search box and type **power plan**.

2. Click Choose a Power Plan in the results list. The Power Options window appears.

3. Click Tell Me More About Power Plans to learn more about what goes into a power plan.

4. Drag the slider to change the screen brightness. (The lower the brightness, the more power you are saving.)

5. Click Change Plan Settings to change the power settings of your current plan.

Screen's So Bright I Gotta Wear Shades

An easy way to adjust the brightness on the fly in Windows 10 is to click the power tool in the system tray and click the Brightness control in the lower-left corner of the pop-up box. Clicking the tool cycles through brightness settings in increments of 25; for example, if you click the tool when the setting is 100% brightness, the setting drops to 25%, and then with each click it increases to 50% and 75% before returning to 100%.

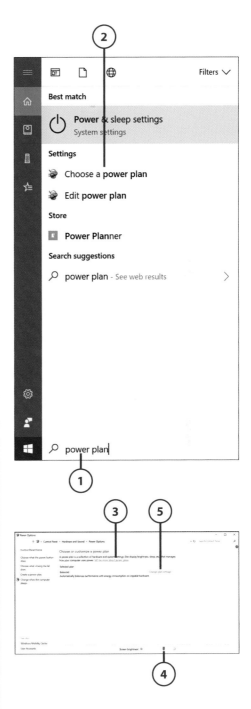

6. Choose when you want Windows 10 to turn off the display when your computer is not in use. You can choose different settings for battery power or plugged-in mode.

7. Select when you want the computer to go to sleep after a period of non-use.

8. Adjust the sliders to the level of brightness you want for battery or plugged-in mode.

9. Click Save Changes.

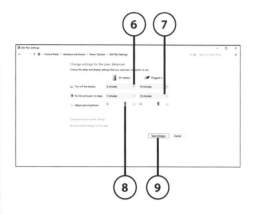

Wait, Reverse That

If you change the power settings and then have second thoughts and want to undo your changes, you can click the Restore Default Settings for This Plan link that appears in the same window where you modify the plan settings. Windows 10 returns the plan to its default settings.

Resetting Windows 10

We all know—only too well—that computers sometimes have their off days. Things slow to a crawl. Your apps hang. Programs aren't launching the way they should.

If you're having problems consistently, Windows 10 gives you a tool that can make things better quickly and easily. Now, instead of crossing your fingers and rebooting—or perhaps arbitrarily choosing a Restore Point and hoping your journey back in time will fix the trouble you're having—you can use Windows Reset to refresh your Windows 10 installation without wiping away any files or settings.

>>>Go Further

HEADACHE-FREE RESETS

One of the big changes behind-the-scenes in Windows 10 is the way the operating system uses and releases storage space to make Windows 10 less draining on hard drives and easier to reset if the computer experiences problems.

Now because of the more efficient way Windows 10 works in the background, you're able to use Reset if you encounter bizarre Windows 10 behaviors; the operating system can rebuild the needed files quickly, and your system is up and running much faster than it would have been in previous releases of Windows.

Resetting Your PC

If you find that a few of your apps aren't working the way they should, or your computer has been behaving unreliably, you can reset your computer to restore the program files and settings to their original state without losing your files, media, and settings.

1. Click the Start button to display the Start menu.

2. Click Settings.

3. Select Update and Security.

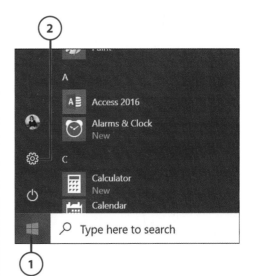

4. Click Recovery.

5. In the Reset This PC area, click the Get Started button if you want to reset your PC and reinstall Windows. You can choose whether you want to keep your files or have Windows remove them and start over.

6. In the Advanced Startup area, click Restart Now to start Windows from a USB drive or DVD, to change your startup settings, or to restore your files from a system image you've previously saved.

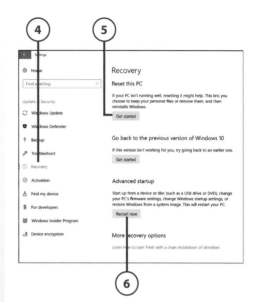

Rolling Back Windows 10

You might see a third option in the Recovery screen of the Settings window: Go Back to the Previous Version of Windows 10. This choice will appear for you only if you've recently installed Windows 10; after 31 days, the files in the Windows.old folder will be overwritten and your previous version of Windows is no longer available. This option is helpful if you have recently installed or upgraded Windows 10 and are having problems with the software; rolling back the installed version and reinstalling will hopefully clear the problems.

>>>Go Further

USING THE WINDOWS MOBILITY CENTER

If you are looking for one central location where you can find the settings that control the way you use your computer on the road, you can go to the Windows Mobility Center. You display the center by clicking in the Search box on the task bar and typing **mobility**. Tapping or clicking the app opens the Windows Mobility Center window.

You can change options for Brightness, Volume, Battery Status, Screen Orientation, External Display, Sync Center, and Presentation Settings in the Windows Mobility Center. Simply tap or click the control of the item you want to change and select your choice.

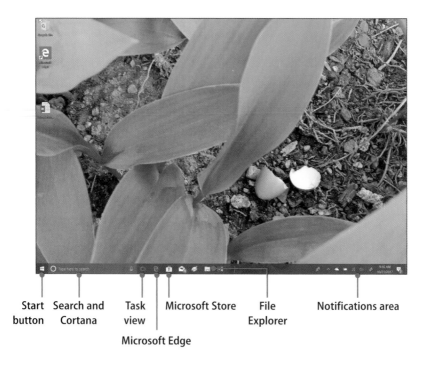

Start   Search and   Task   Microsoft Store   File   Notifications area
button   Cortana   view   Explorer

                                 Microsoft Edge

The Start screen in
Tablet mode

In this chapter, you learn how to find your way around the Windows 10 desktop by performing tasks such as

→ Exploring the Windows 10 desktop
→ Using Tablet mode
→ Tailoring the Taskbar
→ Working with windows
→ Using Task view
→ Working with Notifications and the Action Center
→ Using Ink with Windows 10
→ Creating and using multiple desktops

Accomplishing Windows 10 Essential Tasks

Perhaps it's the mark of progressive software in our day and age: Windows 10 anticipates the tools you will need before you need them. Case in point: If you start Windows 10 on your traditional computer or laptop, the operating system knows to display the operating system in Desktop mode, with the Start menu available behind the Windows Start button in the lower-left corner of your screen. If you launch Windows 10 on your tablet or touch device, such as the Surface 4, the software automatically displays Windows 10 in Tablet mode, with the Start screen optimized (with larger tiles and more space) so you can easily get where you want to go using a fingertip or pen. Whether you will be using Windows 10 on a desktop or a touch device—or a combination of both—there are a set of essential tasks you will perform as you launch and use apps, organize your files, check your social media accounts, and communicate with friends, family, and colleagues.

In this chapter, you find out how to do those basic tasks whether you're using a desktop computer or a touch device. You learn how to navigate your way around the interface, work with the Start menu, tweak the taskbar to suit your liking, work with program windows, use a pen with Windows 10, and even create multiple desktops (which sounds complicated but isn't). By the time you finish this chapter, you will know much more about how to navigate the essentials of Windows 10 so that you can get on to the fun stuff.

Exploring the Windows 10 Desktop

If you're using a computer or device connected to a mouse or keyboard, your version of Windows 10 launches directly to the Windows 10 desktop. If you have used a version of Windows prior to Windows 8, you are likely to feel at home here: The majority of the screen is open space, with the Recycle Bin in the upper-left corner, the Start button in the lower-left corner, a search box and taskbar (containing icons for the tools you use often) along the bottom, and on the far right side, the notifications and system tray tools.

Learning About the Windows 10 Desktop

By default, the Windows 10 Desktop is designed to optimize your space on the screen so you can find what you need easily and still have plenty of space to work with your open applications. You'll probably spend much of your clicking time in the lower-left corner of the screen; this is where you find the Start menu, the Search box, and the tools you'll use regularly, such as Task view, Microsoft Edge (Microsoft's new browser), File Explorer, the Microsoft Store, and any other apps you pin to the taskbar.

Recycle Bin

The Start button displays the Start menu

Search and Cortana

Taskbar

Microsoft Store
Microsoft Edge

File Explorer

Notifications area

- You'll use the Start button as your command center in Windows 10, launching apps, changing settings, accessing your social media, and more.

- The Search box and Cortana give you two unique and connected ways to find information and items on the Web, on your computer, or in your schedule. Search by default aggregates results from both online and off; Cortana is your personal digital assistant that can listen and act on your voice commands, whether you want to locate information, set an appointment, find a restaurant, or something else.

- Task view enables you to see thumbnails of all your open apps so that you can move directly to the one you want to work with next.

- Microsoft Edge is Microsoft's new browser, a state-of-the-art replacement for Internet Explorer. Edge takes advantage of the latest web technologies to give you a smoother, cleaner browsing experience online.

- File Explorer is the familiar tool you use to organize and manage your files and folders in Windows 10.

- The Microsoft Store is your source for finding and downloading apps of all types, as well as media and more.

- The Notifications area includes the new Notifications tool and displays the Action Center, where you can see any messages Windows 10 has for you. This area also enables you to make changes to your computer on-the-fly; for example, you can check how much battery life you have left, adjust the volume of media playback, adjust your wireless settings, or display the onscreen keyboard.

- The Recycle Bin is where all your deleted files and folders go; while they are stored in the Recycle Bin you can still retrieve them for use.

What Is Cortana?

Cortana is Microsoft's answer to a personal digital assistant, ready to help you with voice commands, searches, reminders, and more. After you enable Cortana, you can say something like, "Cortana, wake me up in 15 minutes," and lean back in your chair for a quick nap. Cortana shares space with the Search tool in Windows 10, and it can assist you on PC, tablet, and phone (where Cortana has resided for some time). Chapter 4, "Using Cortana: Your Personal Digital Assistant," covers more about Cortana.

Using the Windows 10 Start Button

The Windows 10 Start button, in the lower-left corner of the screen, opens the Start menu. Right away, you'll notice that the Windows 10 Start menu isn't your ordinary menu. Microsoft added the best of Windows 8.1 (the updating app tiles) to what folks liked best about the Windows 7 Start menu (the list of programs and the ability to view All Programs with a click of the mouse) and put them together in one customizable menu for Windows 10.

When you click the Start button, the menu opens. On the left side, you see your profile at the top, followed by a list of Most Used apps. Beneath that list is an alphabetical list of all the apps installed on your system.

On the right side of the Start menu, you see colorful app tiles. You can group and arrange these app tiles in any way you like. You can also change the size of some app tiles (if the app developer has enabled this feature). You learn how to work with app tiles on the Start menu later in this chapter.

To work with the Windows 10 Start menu, follow these steps:

1. Click the Start button. The Start menu opens.

2. Review the apps in the Most Used list. You can launch these apps by clicking the one you want to use.

3. Move the cursor to an app tile. The tile highlights. To open the app, click the tile.

>>>*Go Further*

FOR THE ADVENTUROUS: POWER TOOLS

If you know your way around an operating system and want a quick way to access some of the tools you are accustomed to using, you can use the "power user" list of tools to find what you need. To display the list, right-click the Start menu, and a list of choices appears that take you into the inner workings of Windows 10. You can choose from Apps and Features, Mobility Center, Power Options, Event Viewer, System, Device Manager, Network Connections, Disk Management, Computer Management, and Windows PowerShell.

You can also access the Task Manager, Settings, File Explorer, Search, and Run from the power user tools. At the bottom of the list are options that enable you to shut down the computer or sign out and change to a different desktop if you've created multiple desktops in Windows 10. Each of these options takes you to a setting or tool that is discussed at various points throughout this book. But the power user tools list gives you quick access to the tools you might need if you're comfortable finding your own way around in Windows 10.

Using the Start Menu

As you can see, the Windows 10 Start menu tries to give you a simple, graphical way to find what you need while still offering the flexibility and functionality that get you there quickly. Whether you prefer lists or tiles, you can use the items you prefer and skip the ones you don't. That's not a bad system.

Microsoft also knows that to really enjoy and use the operating system in the way it's intended, you need to be able to make it your own. So the Start menu is highly customizable. You can add new app tiles to the Start menu; you can change the size of tiles and control whether they update with new information. You also can group similar tiles and add a group name if you like.

Within the colorful Start menu are several options for the ways you work with your system. You might want to click an app tile to launch a program, point to an item on the Most Used list to display a set of options, change to All Apps view, or put your computer to sleep.

Working with the Start Menu

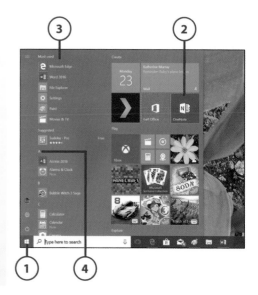

1. Click the Start button. The Start menu appears.

2. Launch an app by clicking the app's tile.

3. Alternatively, click an item in the apps list to launch the tool or app.

4. Open the Start menu again and then click the alphabetical heading to collapse the apps list so you can move quickly to another part of the list.

Jumping Through the Alphabet

To move quickly to a specific app, click the letter in the apps list. This collapses all apps and displays an alphabetical grid so you can click the letter that the app name starts with. After you click the letter, the apps in that letter expand, and you can click the one you want to launch. Simple.

Resizing the Start Menu

Because you are likely to have more favorite apps than those you can display in the Start menu panel by default, Windows 10 gives you the option of expanding the tile area. Simply hover the mouse along the right edge of the open Start menu. When the cursor changes to a double-headed arrow, click and drag the menu to the right, expanding the width of the displayed tile area.

Changing User and Profile Information in the Start Menu

The Start menu displays your Microsoft account profile picture to the left of the apps list. You can interact with your account settings directly by clicking your account picture and choosing Change Account Settings. You can also lock your computer or sign out at that point, if you like.

1. Click the Start button to display the Start menu.

2. Click your profile picture on the left side of the Start menu. A menu appears.

3. Click Change Account Settings if you want to update your Microsoft Account information. This action takes you to the Accounts page of the Settings window, where you can update your account picture or change other items.

4. Click Lock to lock your computer so no one else can access it. (To unlock your computer, sign in using your Microsoft account and password.)

5. To sign out of your computer, click Sign Out.

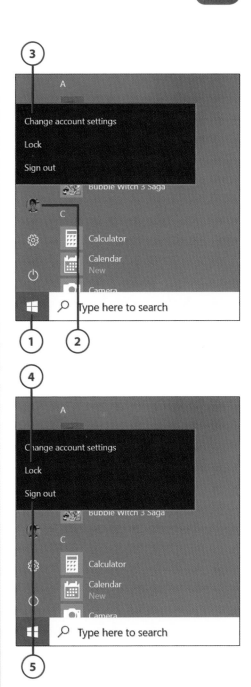

Adding App Tiles to the Start Menu

Although Windows 10 provides a selection of app tiles for you on the Start menu by default, you can add new tiles to the Start menu and arrange them in the way that makes the most sense to you. This enables you to tweak your Start menu so the apps you use most often are easily within your reach.

1. Click the Start button to show the Start menu and the alphabetical listing of all apps installed on your computer.

2. Right-click the app you want to add to the app tiles. An options list appears.

3. Click Pin to Start to add the app as an app tile on the Start menu.

Organizing Apps in Start Menu Folders

A new feature in Windows 10 Creators Update enables you to organize your app tiles in a way that makes sense to you without giving up a lot of real estate on the screen. You can group your apps by creating an app group.

Simply drag and drop one app tile on top of another, and the two will be stored in the same tile on the menu. You'll be able to see small thumbnail versions of the app tiles together in the group. To choose the app you want, simply click or tap the group, and it opens so you can select the app you want to use.

Removing App Tiles from the Start Menu

In addition to adding your own favorite apps to the Start menu, you might want to remove some app tiles you never use. This frees up space for app tiles you'll appreciate having around.

1. Click the Start button to show the Start menu.

2. Right-click the app tile you want to remove.

3. Click Unpin from Start.

Resizing App Tiles

One of the things that makes the Start menu look so inviting is that the app tiles are colorful and dynamic, offering a variety of information—pictures, icons, and some with live updates—all in different sizes. Depending on which app you're working with, you might be able to change the size of the app tile to take up more or less room on the menu.

1. Display the Start menu.

2. Right-click the app tile you want to resize.

3. Click Resize. A list of size options appears.

4. Click the size you want to apply to the selected tile.

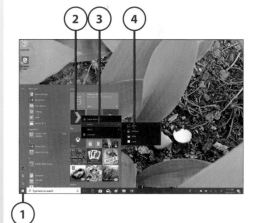

Not All Tiles Are Created Equal

The wrinkle in the mix when it comes to resizing app tiles has to do with what the developer of the app included in the app's capabilities. Some apps have a variety of sizes available, and others have only a few.

Resizing with Touch

If you are using Tablet mode and want to resize your app tiles, press and hold the tile you want to resize. When you see two white circles on the corners of the tile, tap the lower circle. A small options menu appears. Tap Resize and then tap the size you want to assign the file from the submenu that appears.

Turning Off Live Tile Updates

Some of the app tiles in your Start menu have the capability to update information as new content becomes available. You can see this, for example, on the Money app tile, which shows an image and a headline from the most recent article posted in that app. Likewise, your weather app shows you a picture or icons forecasting weather for the near future. Additionally, app tiles such as Mail and Calendar display helpful information, such as the number of new email messages you've received or upcoming appointments in your daily calendar. If you find the updates distracting, you can turn them off so that Windows 10 displays colorful, but static, tiles.

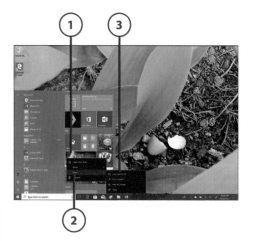

1. Show the Start menu and right-click the app tile you want to change live tile status for.

2. Click More to display additional choices.

3. Click Turn Live Tile Off. The app tile displays an icon and the name of the tile but no longer shows an image or updating information.

Getting the Tiles Going Again

You can turn live tiles back on again by right-clicking them and choosing Turn Live Tile On. Note, however, that not all app tiles are live tiles; this option is available only for those tiles that have Live Tile capabilities programmed into the app.

Using Tablet Mode

If you have a 2-in-1 tablet or you dock your tablet and connect it to a keyboard and mouse, you might be switching back and forth from Desktop to Tablet mode often. In most cases, Windows 10 makes this change automatically for you. When you undock the tablet or flip the screen to use your 2-in-1 as a tablet, Windows 10 adjusts itself so that the touch-optimized features are available. You can specify whether you want Windows 10 to make that change instantly or whether you want to be prompted before the change is made.

You can also manually choose Tablet mode, which is handy if you're using a 2-in-1 device but want to navigate by touch (whether or not the keyboard is active).

Making the Change Manually

Windows 10 should make the change to Tablet mode as soon as you undock your computer. The operating system recognizes that you've "gone mobile" and puts the touch optimization features in place. Depending on which setting you've selected, you might see a notification in the bottom-right corner of your screen, asking whether you want to switch to Tablet mode. You also have the option to switch your computer to Tablet mode manually. Here's how to do that.

1. On the Windows 10 Desktop, tap the Notifications icon in the system tray to display the Action Center.

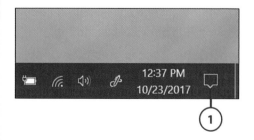

2. Tap Tablet Mode. The Start menu changes to display a grid of app tiles on the screen, and Windows 10 is now in Tablet mode.

Using the Start Menu with Touch

When you're using a tablet, the Windows 10 Start menu appears as a screen-wide grid of tiles so that you easily can choose what you want to use. Even though the interface looks a bit different, all Windows 10 tools and techniques are available to you by touch.

1. Tap the Expand button to display a list of tools for working with Windows 10 in tablet mode.

2. Tap All Apps to display the list of apps installed on your device.

3. Tap Pinned Tiles to return to the app tiles display on the Start screen.

4. Tap Power to shut down the tablet, put it to sleep, or restart it.

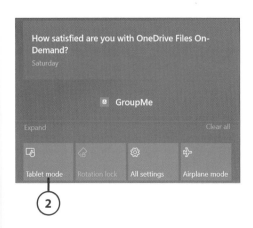

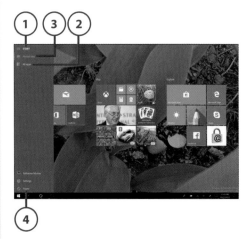

My Desktop Is Blank

After you finish working with an app and close it, you may find yourself looking at a blank desktop. To display the Start menu and the Expand button that goes along with it, tap the Start button in the lower-left corner of the screen. The Start menu appears, offering you all your familiar app tiles, and you can tap the Expand button to display the left column of the Start menu so you can choose from among the apps that don't appear as tiles on the menu.

Tweaking the Start Menu with Touch

You can easily tweak the Start menu to better fit the way you like to work. At the top of the All Apps list on the Start menu, you see the Most Used list. You can remove items from that list or add apps to it. You can also add app tiles to the Start menu and the taskbar to further personalize your Start experience.

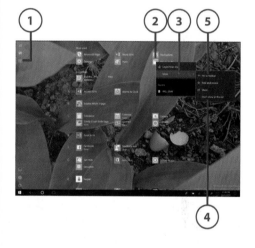

1. Tap the All Apps tool to display all your installed apps in the Start screen area.

2. Tap and hold an item on the Most Used list that you'd like to remove. A context menu appears.

3. Tap More.

4. To remove the item from the list, choose Don't Show in This List.

5. To add the item to the taskbar, tap Pin to Taskbar.

Setting Tablet Mode Options

You can choose a number of preferences for the way in which Windows 10 behaves when you either undock a tablet or switch your device to Tablet mode. You'll find the preferences in the Tablet Mode tab of the System Settings.

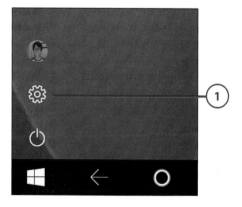

1. Tap the Settings tool just above the Power tool on the far-left edge of the Start screen. The Settings window opens.

2. Tap System.

3. Tap Tablet Mode. In the center of the window, you see four tablet settings.

4. To choose which mode your computer uses when you sign in, tap the down arrow and select Use Tablet Mode, Use Desktop Mode, or leave Use the Appropriate Mode for My Hardware selected. (It's the default.)

5. To choose whether you are prompted before Tablet mode is activated, tap the down arrow and choose Don't Ask Me and Don't Switch, Always Ask Me Before Switching, or Don't Ask Me and Always Switch.

6. If you want app icons on the taskbar to be hidden when you're working in Tablet mode, slide the selection to On.

7. If you want to hide the taskbar when you're working in Tablet mode, slide the selection to On.

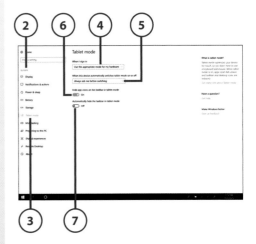

Edge Gestures for Tablets

Because touch is so important for devices running Windows 10, another new feature makes the most of touchable areas on the screen. You can use the new edge gestures to display helpful tools and perform common actions. Here's what the different gestures do:

- Swiping down in a short motion from the top of the screen, if performed on the left or right side of the screen, places the open app in a frame and splits the screen with other open apps.

- Swiping down in a long motion from the top of the screen closes the open app.

- Swiping in from the right side of the screen displays the Action Center.

- Swiping up from the bottom of the screen displays the taskbar if it is hidden from view.

- Swiping in from the left side of the screen displays Task view, showing all open and available apps.

Tailoring the Taskbar

The taskbar is a place for lots of activity on the Windows 10 desktop. By default, just to the right of the Search box, you'll find several icons: Task view, Microsoft Edge, File Explorer, and Microsoft Store. You can start these programs by clicking or tapping those icons.

You can also add apps you use often to the desktop taskbar so you can launch them. For example, if you record audio notes often, you might want to add Sound Recorder to the taskbar; if you work with illustrations, you could add Windows Paint. Any app you use regularly is a good candidate for the Windows 10 taskbar.

Adding Apps to the Taskbar

Some people prefer to put their favorite apps in the taskbar where they are easily within reach. You might think the Start menu serves the same purpose, but if you can save a click of the mouse, why not? The process is simple. Begin by right-clicking the app tile of the app you want to add.

1. Click Start to display the Start menu.

2. In either the All Apps list or the app tiles area, right-click the app that you want to add to the task-bar.

3. Point to More.

4. Click or tap Pin to Taskbar.

Unpinning, After the Fact

If you want to remove a pinned item from the taskbar, right-click it and select Unpin This Program from Taskbar. Instantly it's gone—like it was never even there.

Using Jump Lists

Jump lists are popular features in Windows that enable you to get right to documents and files you've worked with recently without opening menus or launching new programs. A jump list keeps track of the most recent files you've worked with in a program you've pinned to the taskbar. You can display the list by right-clicking the icon on the taskbar. You can then click the file you want and move right to it.

Jump Lists in Start

As you saw earlier in this chapter, Windows 10 also enables you to go directly to jump lists for certain programs that are listed in the Most Used list of the Start menu. You can point to an item in the list and right-click, and the short list appears over the menu so that you can click the item you need.

1. Display the taskbar on the Windows 10 desktop.

2. Right-click the program icon to display the jump list for that program.

3. To open one of the files in the jump list, click or tap the one you want to view.

Jump List Display

If you have only a few files in your jump list, the files appear as thumbnails; when you have a whole slew of files (the default setting in Jump List Properties is 10), you see a list of files instead of thumbnails.

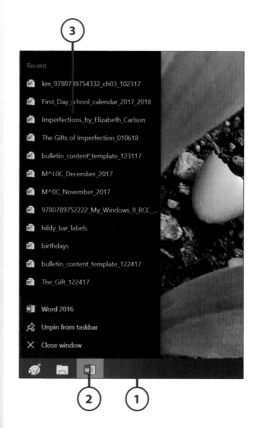

Working with Windows

When you work with programs on the Windows 10 desktop, they appear in the windows you are familiar with if you've used previous versions of Windows. You can open, close, minimize, maximize, arrange, and resize the windows. You can also click or tap the title bar of the window and move it from place to place, and you can arrange more than one window on the screen at the same time.

Window Basics

The windows you open on the Windows 10 desktop have a number of elements in common:

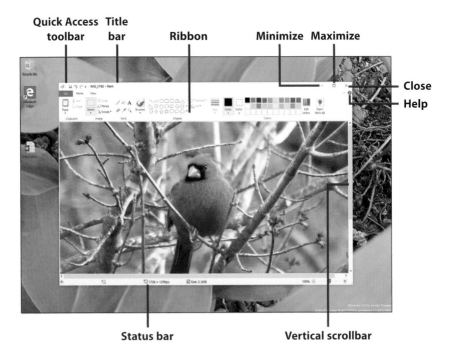

| Quick Access toolbar | Title bar | Ribbon | Minimize | Maximize |

Close
Help

Status bar   Vertical scrollbar

- The title bar displays the name of the program and may display the name of the open file.

- The Minimize, Maximize, and Close buttons control the size of the window. Minimize reduces the window to the taskbar; Maximize opens the window so that it fills the screen; and Close closes the window.

- The Quick Access toolbar gives you access to commands you might want to use with the program. You can customize the Quick Access toolbar by clicking the arrow on the right and selecting additional commands from the list.

- Click the Help button to display help information related to the program you are using.

- The Ribbon tabs offer different sets of tools related to the tasks you're likely to want to perform in the program.

- Click the Minimize Ribbon tool to reduce the display of the ribbon so that only the tab names show. When the Ribbon is hidden, the tool changes to Expand the Ribbon.

- You can click and drag the window border to resize the window.

Moving a Window

Moving a window is as simple as clicking and dragging a window in the direction you want it to go. You can position the window where you want it manually, or you can use a tool to arrange the windows in an orderly way. (You find out how to do that in the next section.)

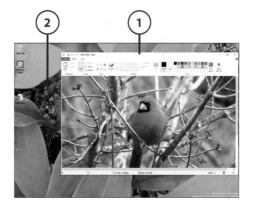

1. Tap and drag—or click and drag—the window's title bar.

2. Drag the window in the direction you want to move it, and release it in the new position.

Resizing a Window

The easiest way to resize a window, from small to large, is to use the Maximize button in the window controls in the upper-right corner of the window. You can also resize a window by positioning the pointer on the window border or corner and dragging in the direction you want to resize the window.

1. Tap or point to a corner or side of the window. The pointer changes to a double-headed arrow.

2. Drag the border in the direction you want to resize the window, and release the border (or the mouse button) when the window is the size you want it.

Switching to a Different Window

While you're working on the desktop, you can easily have many windows open onscreen at once. These windows might be program windows or folders of files. If you work with a number of programs open at one time, you need to be able to get to the program you want when you need it. If several windows are open on the screen, you can click any part of the window you want to bring it to the top, or you can click the taskbar icon of the window you want to view. Alternatively, you can click the Task View tool to the right of the Search box in the taskbar. This displays all open apps in Thumbnail view so that you can click the one you want to work with next.

Arranging Windows

Another important task when you are working with multiple open windows at one time is having the capability to arrange the windows the way you want them to appear. If you want to compare two documents, for example, it would be nice to show them side by side. You can arrange windows the way you want on the Windows 10 desktop.

1. Right-click the taskbar and select Cascade Windows.

2. Right-click the taskbar and select Show Windows Stacked.

3. Right-click the taskbar and click Show Windows Side by Side.

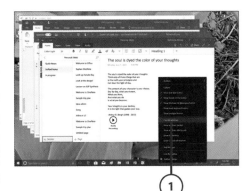

>>>*Go Further*

SHORTCUT KEYS FOR WINDOW WRANGLING

You can also work with the windows on your desktop without ever taking your hands off the keyboard. Here are the shortcut keys you can use:

- Windows+Plus Sign (+) on the numeric keypad zooms in on the current window.

- Windows+Minus Sign (–) zooms out on the current window.

- Windows+Up Arrow maximizes the current window.

- Windows+Down Arrow restores or minimizes the current window.

- Windows+M minimizes all open windows.

- Windows+E opens the Quick Access folder in File Explorer.

- Windows+D displays the desktop.

Quick-Changing Windows

You can change the size of a window quickly by double-clicking (or double-tapping) the title bar. If the window was full-screen size (that is, maximized), it returns to its earlier smaller size. If the window is smaller than full screen, double-clicking the title bar maximizes it.

Old-Style Resizing

Sure, all these double-click tricks are fancy and fast. But if you prefer to choose commands from menus, you can display a window's control panel and select the command you want—Restore, Move, Size, Minimize, and Close—from the list of options. You can find the control panel for the window in the upper-left corner; you can't miss it because it resembles a small program icon (in Word, you see a Word icon; in Excel, you see an Excel icon; and so forth).

Using Task View

Windows 10 also includes a view called Task view, which enables you to navigate quickly among open apps so that you can choose which one you want to work with next. This serves as a simple alternative to Alt+Tab, which cycles through open apps so that you can select the one you need. Task view, by contrast, shows all the open apps as thumbnails on the screen at one time so you can easily choose the one you want.

Displaying and Using Task View

The tool you need for displaying Task view is just to the right of the Search box on the Windows 10 taskbar.

1. Click the Task View tool in the taskbar. Your open apps appear as thumbnails in the center of the screen.

2. Click the image of the application you want to use.

3. Alternatively, hover the mouse over the right corner of an application image to display the Close box, and click the Close box to exit the app.

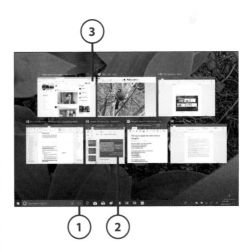

Working with Notifications and the Action Center

Another feature you're likely to use often in Windows 10 is the Notifications tool, which opens the Action Center along the right side of the screen. You'll notice that notifications also slide in from the right toward the bottom of the screen—announcing their presence with a chime—whenever a new file is posted to the cloud, you plug in a new device, you miss a phone call, or a setting needs your attention.

The Notifications tool resembles a small speech balloon, and it appears on the far-right side of the taskbar. When you click the Notifications tool, the Action Center panel opens, listing all the notifications in various apps and settings. At the bottom of the Notifications panel, you have access to various system settings, which enable you to tailor the functioning of your computer easily without going through the Start menu to display the Settings window.

Checking Notifications

Windows 10 lets you know when a new notification arrives by displaying a small rectangular message box in the lower-right corner of the screen. In Windows 10 2017 Fall Creators Update, you can see a small number indicating how many new notifications you have received. You can also click the Notifications tool at any time to see a list of all recent notifications.

1. Click the Notifications tool in the taskbar. The Action Center opens on the right side of the screen.

2. Review the list of notifications.

3. To act on a notification, click it, and a window opens taking you to the app that needs your attention.

4. Remove a notification you no longer need by hovering the mouse over the down arrow on the right side. A close box appears above the arrow. Click the X to remove the notification.

5. To delete all notifications, click Clear All.

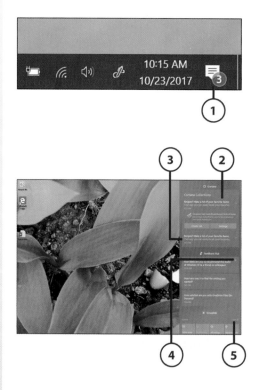

Turning Notifications Off and On

If you find the notifications distracting (or the sound annoying), you can turn off notifications for a period of time while you focus on the task at hand.

1. Right-click the Notifications tool in the taskbar. A small context menu appears.

2. Click Turn on Quiet Hours. When you're ready to turn on notifications again, click Turn Off Quiet Hours.

Reducing Notification Clutter

You can make a few other changes to your notifications if you want to be interrupted less as you work. Choose Don't Show Number of New Notifications or Don't Show App Icons to turn off the number or the source of the notifications you receive.

Using Ink with Windows 10

Windows 10 has been designed from the ground up to allow you to use the software in whatever way—and on whatever device—feels most comfortable for you. Now in Windows 10 2017 Fall Creators Update, the Ink feature has been dramatically improved. Not only can you easily use a pen to write, draw, and select items on the screen, but in many cases you can also simply use your finger to draw, highlight, and add other enhancements on the fly.

Getting Ready to Use Ink

If you have a pen, Windows 10 will likely recognize that by default. But if you don't see the Windows Ink Workspace tool on the right side of your taskbar, you can turn it on by right-clicking the taskbar and clicking the Show Windows Ink Workspace button.

Displaying the Windows Ink Workspace

The Windows Ink Workspace tool is in the notifications area on the right side of the taskbar. When you click or tap the tool, the Windows Ink Workspace opens.

1. Click or tap the Windows Ink Workspace tool.

2. Choose the tool you want to use. Windows Ink Workspace gives you the choice of creating a sticky note, using the sketch pad, or capturing and annotating a picture of your computer screen.

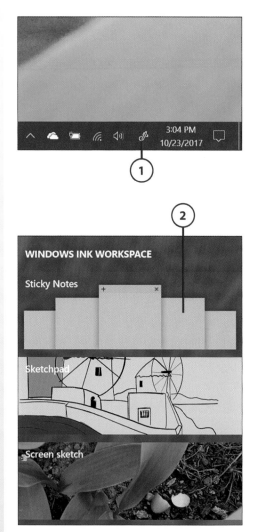

Drawing with Ink

Because the other two tools in the Windows Ink Workspace—Sketchpad and Screen Sketch—have to do with drawing, you'll find more about those tools in Chapter 11, "Bringing Out Your Inner Artist with Photos and Paint 3D."

Creating a Sticky Note

Windows Ink enables you to easily add sticky notes in places you need reminders—perhaps you want to remind yourself that it's your day to pick the kids up from soccer or that you need 20 copies of your PowerPoint presentation for tomorrow's board meeting.

1. Click Sticky Notes in the Windows Ink Workspace (not shown). A sticky note appears in the center of your screen.

2. Using your pen or your finger, write the item you want to remember on the note.

3. Click or tap the Menu button to change the color of the note.

4. Click Add Note if you want to create another sticky note.

5. Click or tap Delete Note to delete the sticky note. Windows 10 asks you to confirm that you want to delete the note; click Delete to remove it.

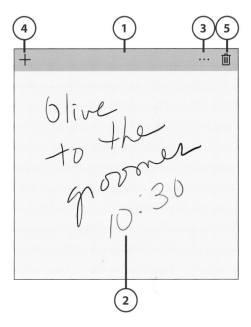

Setting Reminders

If you write a specific time on your sticky note, the text for the time changes color. This happens because Windows 10 recognizes what you wrote as a time, which means you might want to add it to your calendar and set a reminder so you won't forget.

1. Display the sticky note with the time you want to set a reminder for.

2. Tap the time. A small options bar opens at the bottom of the note.

3. Tap Add Reminder. Windows 10 opens the Cortana panel, giving you several options for setting the reminder.

4. Tap to choose when you want to be reminded.

5. Tap and select how often you want to be reminded.

6. Tap or click Remind to save the reminder.

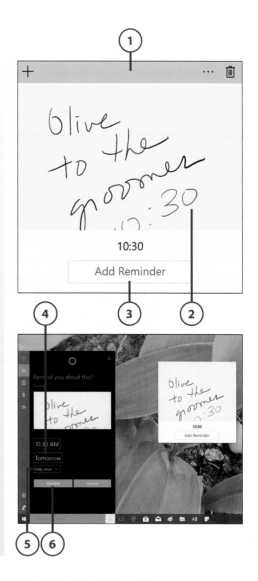

Creating and Using Multiple Desktops

Another exciting feature in Windows 10 that is getting a lot of attention is its multiple desktops. Now you can easily create separate desktops to organize tasks, projects, and apps for different uses. For example, you might want to create one desktop for "work" and one for "home." You can create two desktops and put the apps you use in each of those places on the different desktops. Then when you get home, or you get to work, you can simply display the desktop you want to use and have all your favorite apps right there.

Creating a New Desktop

Creating a new desktop is as simple as a click. Here's the process:

1. Display Task view by clicking the Task View tool in the desktop taskbar.

2. Click New Desktop. The desktop appears as a thumbnail along the bottom of the screen. The top of the desktop is blank because you need to add the apps you want to use to the desktop.

Desktop Creation Shortcut
You can also create a new desktop with a shortcut key combination: Windows+Ctrl+D.

Adding Apps to the New Desktop

After you create the new desktop, you need to add the apps you want to use there. You can use Task view to determine which desktop is active and move the apps you want to use on the new desktop.

1. Display Task view by clicking the tool in the desktop taskbar. As you can see, open apps appear in the center of the screen, and your desktops appear at the bottom of the screen. Make sure the original desktop is selected.

2. Right-click the app in the original desktop you want to move to the new desktop.

3. Point to Move To.

4. Choose Desktop 2. The selected app is moved to the second desktop.

Chapter 3

Switching Among Desktops

You can move back and forth between multiple desktops by using Task view and clicking the desktop you want to use or by pressing Windows+Ctrl+left arrow or Windows+Ctrl+right arrow.

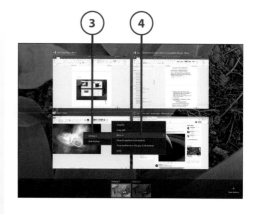

Closing a Desktop

When you're ready to do away with a desktop you've created, you can remove it as easily as you would close a file.

1. Click Task view to display the open apps and desktops.

2. Hover the mouse over the desktop you want to close.

3. Click the Close box to close the desktop.

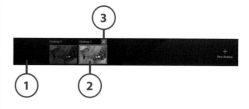

Cortana can find, store, and give
you directions to restaurants
with your favorite cuisine.

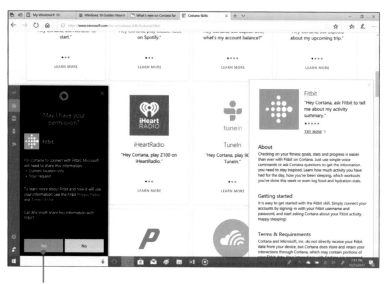

Cortana skills help you
get and share data with
apps and devices you use
throughout your day.

This chapter shows you how Cortana can help personalize and streamline your computing experience by demonstrating these tasks:

→ Getting started with Cortana

→ Searching with Cortana

→ Using Cortana's notebook

→ Adding to Cortana's skills

→ Setting tasks with Cortana

→ Having Cortana find your phone

→ Managing Cortana permissions

4

Using Cortana: Your Personal Digital Assistant

Windows 10 Fall Creators Update has given Cortana a big boost. Although it first appeared as a functional assistant on Windows Phone, Cortana's early skills have been greatly expanded so that now it can help you find information, make connections, and save the things that interest you, no matter what app you are using or what kind of information you seek.

Cortana now does a whole lot more than it used to. You can simply talk to it and use voice comments to ask questions, such as, "Is the movie *Marshall* good?" Cortana will respond with the average rating for the movie (out of 10 stars) and give you links to more information, including directions to the nearest theater where the movie is playing.

Cortana also helps you schedule appointments, figure out a song you heard on the radio, decide whether to wear a coat today, and much more.

Cortana reduces the need to do a lot of typing as you look for information. You can simply say, "Hey Cortana!" and then ask the question or give the command you want Cortana to help you with. If that sounds too good to be true, try it a few times. Here are some of the tasks Cortana can do for you:

- Open an app you want to use
- Give you the current weather
- Tell you the latest sports scores
- Read the headlines
- Find (and tell you about) top recipes
- Put your computer to sleep
- Locate the nearest Thai restaurant (and provide the directions to get you there)
- Tell you a joke
- Set an alarm so you can have a quick nap
- Remind you of an upcoming event
- Increase or decrease the volume of your PC or device
- Keep track of your Microsoft account and your profile information
- Store information about your favorite places (stores, restaurants, and more)
- Play a game with you (try saying, "Play movie game")
- Tell you some trivia you can use to impress friends at a party
- Help you find the name of the song you like (just give it a few of the lyrics)
- Do quick number conversions
- Play a song in your Groove Music app
- Track packages that are being shipped to you

Getting Started with Cortana

For the most part, Cortana works right off the bat without a whole lot of intervention from you. Your computer does need to have a microphone if you plan to use voice commands, of course, and if you want to wake Cortana up by calling its name, you need to change a setting so that can happen.

Is This Thing On?

You can check to make sure Cortana will hear you by displaying Settings, choosing Cortana, and clicking Talk to Cortana. Click the Check the Microphone link at the top of the page. The Speech Wizard launches and walks you through a series of steps, including repeating a phrase so the microphone can check the function and sound level of your microphone. When Windows 10 tells you everything is working properly, you're ready to speak to Cortana.

Leaving a Wake-up Call

Turn on the "Hey Cortana" feature so that Cortana hears you talking and activates the Search box to the right of the Windows 10 Start button.

1. Click or tap in the Search box.

2. Click or tap Settings. The Talk to Cortana page of the Cortana settings appears.

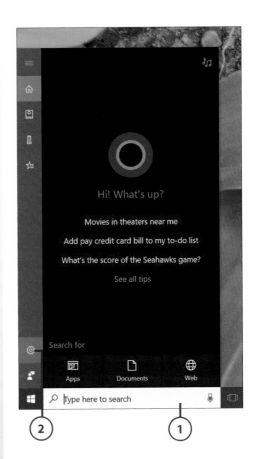

3. Set the Hey Cortana setting to the On position.

4. If you want to be able to keep your computer from sleeping so you can use "Hey Cortana" whenever your computer is plugged in, click this check box.

5. Choose whether you want Cortana to respond to anyone who says "Hey Cortana" or only to you.

Keys, Not Commands

If you'd rather use a shortcut key than a voice command to activate Cortana's abilities, slide the Keyboard Shortcut setting to the On position. This enables you to put Cortana into "listening mode" by pressing Windows+C.

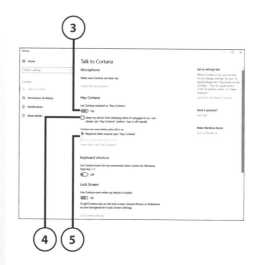

Cortana on Your New System

If you've just purchased a new computer or device that is running Windows 10 Fall Creators Update, Cortana is there to walk you through the process of setting up your system.

Cortana explains each step of the process and asks you to answer "Yes" or "No" as it sets up the various options to get you going. You can ask questions along the way, and Cortana responds in kind. If you'd rather not have your computer talking to you while you're going through the setup process, you can always click the sound icon to mute Cortana.

Learning the Cortana Tools

When you click or tap in the Search box to the right of the Windows Start button, the Cortana panel opens. Along the left side of the panel, you see several tools. To learn the name of each of the tools, you can click the Expand tool at the top of the tools row.

1. Tap Home to see a mix of current information tailored to your local area, including weather conditions, top headlines, nearby restaurants, and more.

2. Tap Cortana's Notebook to see an overview of what you have planned for today, as well as favorite places, traffic conditions, restaurants, headlines, and more.

3. Tap Devices if you have an Invoke speaker designed specifically to work with Cortana. (Think of Amazon's Alexa speaker.) Cortana leads you through the setup process.

4. Tap Collections to see favorites you've saved in Books, Movies & TV, Recipes, Restaurants, and Shopping.

5. Tap Settings to see and change Cortana settings as needed.

6. Tap Feedback to send Microsoft your thoughts and suggestions about Cortana.

Searching with Cortana

Once you've set up Cortana to hear you when you say, "Hey Cortana," you can ask for help in searching for anything. You can also ask a variety of other questions that can help you organize and manage your day. Phrase your question in a regular sentence-style question; Cortana asks for more information if it doesn't understand.

So What Is Microsoft Listening In On?

The user agreement language for Cortana tells you that Microsoft needs your permission to collect and use your location information, as well as data about your contacts, your voice input, information from your email messages and texts, your browser history and search history, your calendar details, and other information. Surely they need your shoe size, too? In this day and age, collecting too much information makes some users wary, and that's understandable. But Microsoft is gathering usage data (and no doubt will be marketing products in a way that makes good use of that data), and if you don't mind the company being up front about it, click I Agree and start having fun with Cortana.

You can take a look at the information Cortana is collecting by clicking Settings in the navigation bar on the left of the Cortana panel and then clicking Permissions & History. Click the Change What Cortana Knows About Me in the Cloud link to review the interests, places, search history, and more information Cortana has collected and saved to personalize your experience.

Seek and Find with Cortana

When you're ready to search for something, you can wake Cortana up by saying, "Hey Cortana!" Or, if you prefer (if someone is listening on the other side of the cubicle wall), you can click in the Search box and type the word or phrase you're looking for.

1. Say, "Hey Cortana!" or click the microphone icon on the right side of the Search box. (If Cortana doesn't respond to your voice, click the Settings tool in Cortana and make sure the Hey Cortana slider is set to On.)

Speak up!

After you've turned on the Hey Cortana setting so the tool is able to respond to your voice commands, Windows might prompt you to set up your microphone. If you see the Set Up Your Mic message box, click Next, read the sentences the prompt displays, and click Finish to complete setting up your microphone. Cortana should now be ready for your voice commands.

2. When you see Listening displayed in the box, tell Cortana what to search for (for example, "Find a Thai restaurant nearby").

What's That?

If Cortana isn't hearing you properly, click the small microphone tool on the right side of the Search box. This opens the Cortana tool, and you can tell Cortana what you're looking for.

3. Cortana instantly displays a results page with a selection of search results that match what you're searching for. Click the result that looks most promising.

4. Click the map if you want to use the Maps app to find the route to the location.

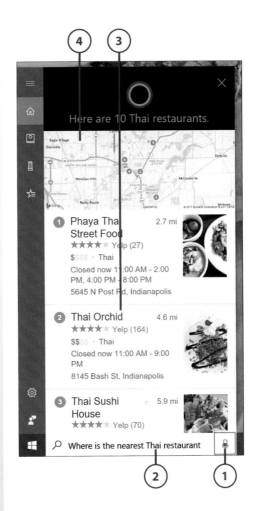

Cortana: A Fount of Knowledge

You aren't limited with Cortana to searching for restaurants or looking for car reviews. You can ask Cortana what the weather will be like in Des Moines tomorrow afternoon, suggest that it find the best prices for mid-sized rental cars, or even ask it to find a new ringtone for your phone. Experiment with Cortana and find out how helpful it can be to you. After you get over the awkwardness of speaking to your computer screen, it's rather fun.

Using Cortana's Notebook

The benefits of having a digital personal assistant like Cortana go beyond simply finding information on things you're curious about. Cortana also has a notebook in which it collects resources and data related to more than a dozen different topics. You'll find that you can locate and customize information gathered in each of the following topic areas:

- About me
- Lists
- Reminders
- Collected services
- Music
- Connected home
- Skills
- Cortana tips
- Eat & drink
- Finance
- Getting around

- Meetings & reminders
- News
- Packages
- Pick up where I left off
- Shopping
- Special days
- Sports
- Suggested reminders
- Travel
- Weather

Exploring the Cortana Notebook

The Notebook is in the Cortana tools along the left side of the Cortana panel.

1. Click or tap in the Search box. The Cortana panel opens.

2. Tap the Notebook tool. A list of topics appears.

3. Drag the scrollbar to review the entire list.

4. Tap or click the topic you'd like to explore.

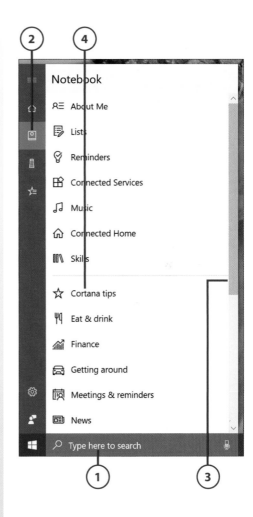

Personalizing Cortana's Info

You'll notice that the various categories in the Cortana Notebook need more information from you before the results shown there will be very helpful. For example, if you click the Sports topic in the Notebook, you'll see the settings Cortana has in place for that choice as well as a link that invites you to add your own favorite teams so Cortana can track them for you.

1. Click in the Search box and tap Notebook to display Cortana's categories.

2. Click or tap the Eat & Drink category and scroll down.

3. Tap the Add a Cuisine link. A list of cuisine categories appears.

4. Tap or click the categories of cuisine you enjoy.

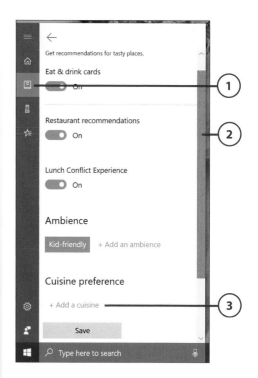

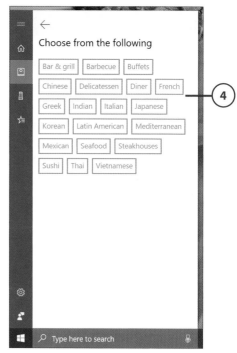

5. Tap the Add button, and Cortana adds the cuisine in the Cuisine Preferences area of the Eat & Drink category.

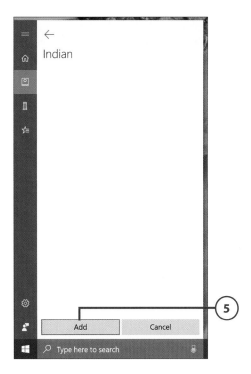

Adding to Cortana's Skills

Cortana skills are new in Windows 10 Fall Creators Update, dramatically expanding what Cortana can help you do, and opening the door for developers all over the world to create voice apps and tasks that Cortana can incorporate.

The first skills available in Cortana had to do with travel, finance, and web-based mail—offered by company names you will recognize—but they were quickly followed by skills for music streaming, ticket purchasing, and restaurant reservations. The list of skills keeps growing. You can find a list of featured skills on the Microsoft website at www.microsoft.com/en-us/cortana/skills/featured.

Expanding Cortana's Skills

The skills are in Cortana's Notebook in the Cortana panel. To get started, you need to add at least one skill to Cortana's capabilities.

1. Click or tap in the Search box or say, "Hey Cortana."

2. Tap the Notebook tool or say, "Open the Notebook."

3. Tap or say, "Skills."

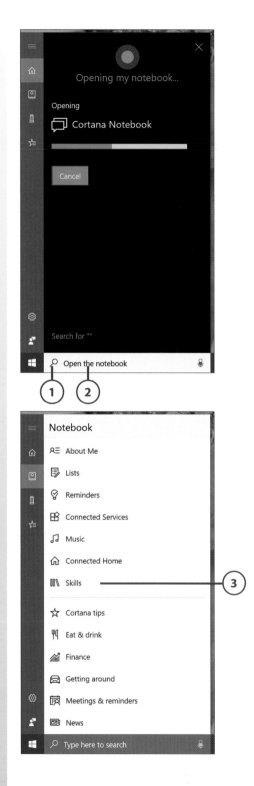

4. Click the Learn More About link. Windows 10 opens the Edge browser and displays a collection of skills you can install.

5. Click the name of a skill you'd like to add. A details panel opens about that skill to provide more information.

6. Say, "Hey Cortana" and read the text just beneath the skill name (in this case, "Ask Fitbit to tell me about my activity summary").

7. When Cortana ask for your permission to access data in the skill you've selected, say, "Yes" or click the Yes button.

8. When prompted, click the Authorize button (or say, "Authorize") to confirm the link between Cortana and the skill app. You can now receive information from that skill by simply asking Cortana about it. In this example, if I say, "Hey Cortana, ask Fitbit to tell me my activity summary," Cortana tells me how many steps I've walked, how many sets of stairs I've climbed, and how many calories I've burned so far today.

New Skills All the Time

Microsoft is counting on developers to create a universe of voice apps for Cortana (and already you can find a healthy number of skills in many different categories, and the number increases continually). Click the link in Cortana skills to review new featured skills periodically for new additions.

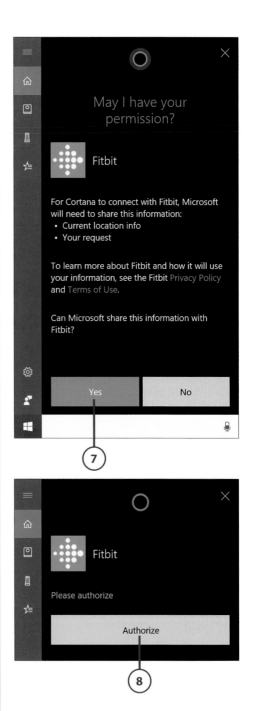

Picking Up Where You Left Off with Cortana

Another slick new Cortana feature in Windows 10 Creators Update enables you to start a task on one computer or device and finish it on another. This might come in handy when you're reading a major article for a presentation you'll be giving later this week, and you don't have time to finish it before it's time to leave.

If you've turned on Cortana's Help Me Pick Up Where I Left Off feature, you can finish the article when you get home (as long as you log into your home computer using the same Microsoft account you were using on the other computer or device). The article appears as a link in your Action Center, bookmarked to the place you left off.

Setting Tasks with Cortana

As you can see, Cortana really is more than a glorified search tool. She is meant to be a personal digital assistant. She can help you with scheduling, research, and more—just like a human assistant might. You can ask Cortana to schedule tasks, create invitations, and more.

1. Click in the Search box or say, "Hey Cortana!" to let the tool know you have a request.

2. Speak the tasks you want Cortana to perform, such as, "Wake me up in 15 minutes."

3. Cortana answers your request telling you what action she has taken.

4. You can edit the task created by clicking or tapping it.

5. Click or tap the slider to turn the alarm off.

6. Edit alarm settings by clicking or tapping the alarm.

7. Tap and hold the alarm to display a delete option; tap Delete to remove it.

Cortana, Your Instant Assistant

Cortana is also available right on your Lock screen. So without even swiping open Windows 10 or typing in the password, you can simply ask, "Hey Cortana, when is my next appointment?" and the tool locates the information and tells you.

Cortana on the Lock screen gives you a number of rotating suggestions for the types of commands or questions you might want to offer. Also be sure to keep Cortana Tips turned on (you can set this in Cortana Settings and also in Cortana Tips in the Notebook) so you continue to get ideas on how to improve and expand the way you work with your personal digital assistant.

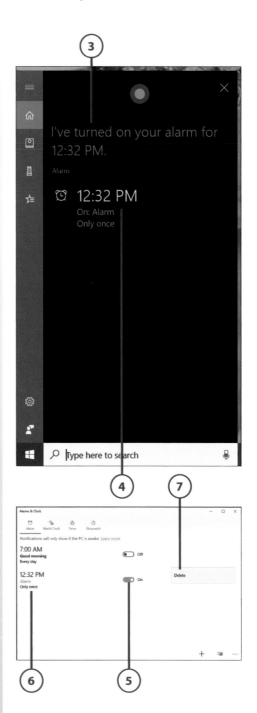

Having Cortana Find Your Phone

Just like a real digital assistant who helps you locate your lost car keys or briefcase, Cortana can help you locate your phone when you lose it.

1. Say, "Hey Cortana!" The Search box becomes active and you see the Listening message.

2. Ask, "Where's my phone?" Cortana responds that it will attempt to find it for you. After a moment or two, you hear a message notification on your phone (if it is within earshot), saying, "Cortana is looking for this phone."

3. When the phone is located, a notification appears, telling you Cortana has found your phone. Click or tap Ring It to send a signal to your phone so that it will ring.

4. Tap or click the map at the top of the notification if you want to use the Maps app to get directions to where Cortana found your phone.

5. Click or tap Dismiss if you were able to find the phone with the notification sound and no longer need the ring signal sent.

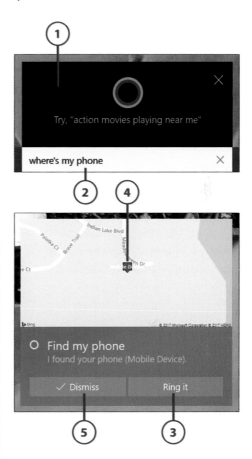

Managing Cortana Permissions

As you can imagine, with a personal digital assistant like Cortana, in order to provide you with information relative to your likes and dislikes, your location, and your interests, Cortana has to know a lot about you. In this day of cyber-security concerns, you need to be able to manage how your information is stored and used.

For that reason, you can choose how you want Cortana to gather information on you and manage how it is used. You do this using Cortana settings.

Managing Your Permissions

Microsoft has been working with a focus on security and privacy across the last several iterations of Windows 10, and the overall security effort is coalescing into an organized permissions-based system. Now your Cortana settings are organized as one part of a large Windows-wide security system designed to give you the flexibility you want to control your information while balancing that with the permissions you need to get to the information you seek.

You can view and change the permissions Cortana uses to search for, display, and update your information by choosing Settings in the Cortana panel.

1. Click in the Search box or say, "Hey Cortana." The Cortana panel opens.

2. Click Settings.

3. Click Permissions & History.

4. Click Change What Cortana Knows About Me in the Cloud to view and modify the types of information Cortana stores about you.

5. Click or tap Manage the Information Cortana Can Access from This Device to limit what Cortana will find and share about your location, communications, and browsing history.

6. Leave this set to on if you want Cortana to be able to display information you've stored in the cloud in searches.

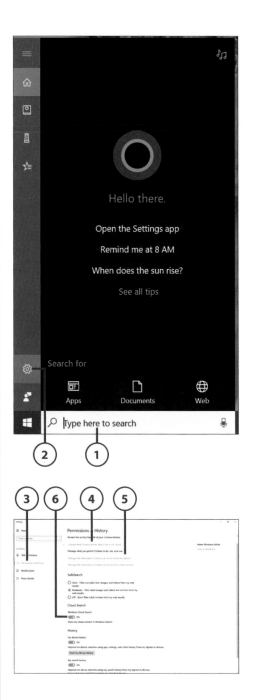

7. Leave My Device History set to On if you want Cortana to learn from past searches and questions on this device about the types of information and topics that interest you.

8. Click or tap Clear My Device History to erase past search data.

9. Set to Off if you want to stop Cortana from keeping a history of your searches.

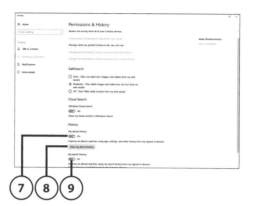

Setting Notifications

One of Cortana's strengths is that it can use notifications to remind you of things you want to be reminded about: upcoming appointments, grocery items, work tasks, and times for the kids' after-school practices. You can control how and when Cortana notifies you about various events in Cortana settings.

1. Display Cortana settings by clicking in the Search box and choosing the Settings tool. In the Settings window, click Notifications.

2. If you want Cortana to send notifications to all your Windows devices (tablet, computer, phone), leave this set to On.

3. If you want Cortana to make suggestions for items you might want to add to your collections (for example, when you search for a specific recipe), leave this set to On.

4. Click Manage Notifications if you want to leave notifications on for some items but turn them off for others. The collection choices are Books, Movies & TV, Recipes, and Shopping. By default, all are turned On.

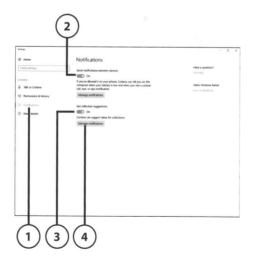

>>>Go Further

LIMITING CORTANA

Because Cortana can potentially add so much to your computing experience—and because she is a seamless part of many of the apps you'll use every day—developers recommend that for the best use of Windows 10, you should let Cortana do what she does best.

But not everyone likes this sort of thing. Unfortunately, in the previous version of Windows 10 (Windows 10 Anniversary Update), Microsoft did away with the option to disable Cortana. So no matter what you do, it continues operating to some degree in the background.

But you can limit the permissions you give Cortana for gathering and storing information about your computing activities. To put a check and balance on Cortana's power, you make changes in Cortana Settings:

- In the Talk to Cortana category, set Hey Cortana to Off and the Lock Screen setting to Off.

- In the Permissions & History category, set Cloud Search, My Device History, and My Search History settings to Off. Click the Clear My Device History button to remove past search data.

- In the Notifications category, set Notification Between Devices and Category Notifications to Off.

You can reverse these settings at any time to restore Cortana to normal functionality. You can also provide feedback to Microsoft (by using the Feedback tool in the Cortana panel) if you want to weigh in on how Cortana stores and uses your information in future updates of Windows 10.

Free Time with Cortana

Like any good assistant, Cortana isn't all work and no play. In fact, you can play games with Cortana (just say, "Hey Cortana, play movie game"), ask Cortana to share some interesting trivia, or even ask it to tell you a joke. Here's the result when I said, "Hey Cortana, tell me a joke." Not bad.

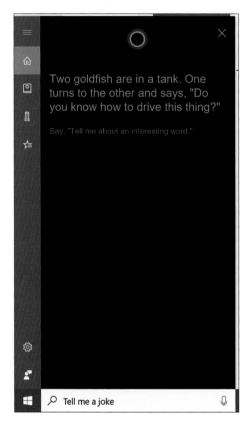

Use Personalization settings
to change the way Windows
10 looks and behaves.

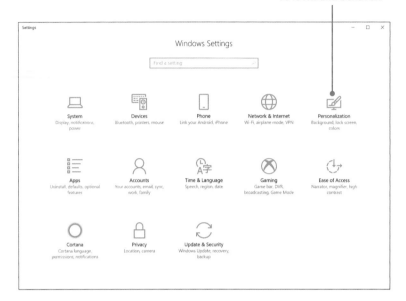

Add a new background or create a
slideshow using your own images.

In this chapter, you learn to change the way Windows 10 looks and acts by doing the following tasks:

→ Selecting a new desktop background
→ Adjusting colors in Windows 10
→ Setting a night light in Windows 10
→ Personalizing the Lock screen
→ Choosing a Windows 10 theme
→ Customizing the Start menu
→ Tweaking additional system settings

Personalizing Windows 10

We live in a time when we can personalize everything. We just like things the way we like them—and Windows 10 is no exception. You can personalize many things about the way Windows 10 operates on your computer or device—changing your screen background, adjusting colors, choosing a visual theme, customizing the way the Start menu behaves, and so on. Now in Windows 10 Fall Creators Update, you can use the new Night Light feature to take the bright blue out of the light when you're using your computer after dark. This makes reading the screen easier on your eyes.

Windows handles some of this customization for you. If you're using a touch device, Windows 10 automatically appears in Tablet mode so that your experience is optimized for touch. If you're using a desktop computer, your Windows 10 shows up to be mouse friendly. You won't have to do anything to choose one or the other.

This chapter shows you how to make these changes to create the Windows 10 experience that's right for you.

Saving Your Changes—Not

You might notice the lack of a Save step in the tasks in this chapter. Yes, it's a little hard to get used to, but for many settings there's no Save button when you make changes to the Personalization settings discussed in this chapter. Windows 10 saves your changes as you work, so you don't need to take a specific action to complete the operation. When you're done, just click or tap the Close button on the active window. If you're one of those people (like me) who likes to wrap things up neatly, not having a Save button is a little disconcerting, but we'll get used to it (hopefully).

Selecting a New Desktop Background

Your Windows 10 Desktop background sets the backdrop for your whole computing experience. You might be surprised to discover what a difference a background makes. Try changing it, and you'll see. Some images are energizing; others are relaxing.

You can use one of the images that are included with Windows 10 or choose photos that have meaning for you. You can also choose a solid color instead of a picture, if you like, or create a slideshow so you can see multiple images instead of just one.

Displaying Personalization Settings

1. Click the Start button to display the Start menu.

2. Click Settings.

3. Click Personalization. The Personalization settings appear. The Background category is selected by default.

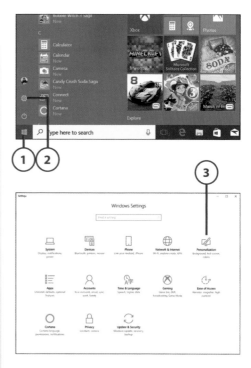

Choosing a New Background Picture

Windows 10 makes it easy for you to substitute a new picture for the image your background currently displays. You can choose an image provided with Windows 10, or you can add one of your own. From the Personalization screen, follow these steps:

1. Click Background (assuming it's not already selected).

2. Click the Background arrow and choose Picture.

3. Click a picture from among the thumbnails displayed.

4. Alternatively, click Browse to find and select a different picture.

5. Click the folder containing the picture you want to use.

6. Select a picture in the right side of the Open dialog box.

7. Click Choose Picture. The picture you have added is applied to the desktop in the Preview window at the top of the Personalization window.

8. Click the Choose a Fit arrow, and choose how you want Windows 10 to place the photo on the desktop. You can choose from Fill, Fit, Stretch, Tile, Center, and Span.

9. Close the Personalization window.

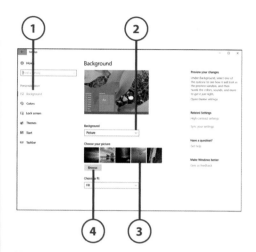

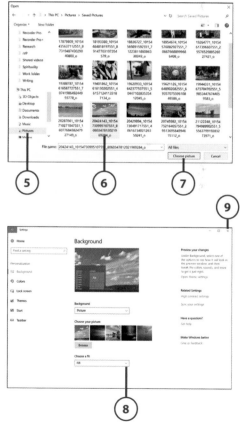

Selecting a Color Background

If you'd rather not use a picture for your desktop background, you can choose a color you like for the Windows 10 backdrop. From the Personalization screen, follow these steps:

1. Click Background if it is not selected.

2. Select Solid Color from the Background list.

3. Click the color you want to apply to the background. The Preview window shows the effect of the change.

4. Click Close to exit Settings when you have selected the color you want.

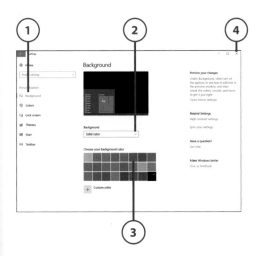

Creating a Custom Color

New in Windows 10 Fall Creators Update, you can create your own custom color for your desktop background. The tool you need is in the Background page of the Personalization settings.

1. Click Background if it is not selected.

2. Click the Custom Color button. You see a pop-up box with palette of colors.

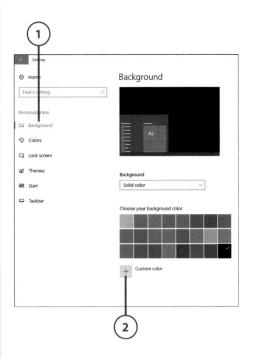

3. Click the color you want to use.

4. Drag the slider to make the color lighter or darker.

5. Click Done to choose the color.

Coloring by Numbers

If you know the numeric value of the color you want to use (for example, the Red-Green-Blue values), click the More link in the Pick a Background Color pop-up box and enter the numeric values for the hues. Click Done to save the custom color to your palette.

Creating a Background Slideshow

You can also create a slideshow for your desktop background so that Windows 10 displays a series of your favorite pictures while you work. To get the step-by-step process, see the section "Creating a Slideshow" later in this chapter.

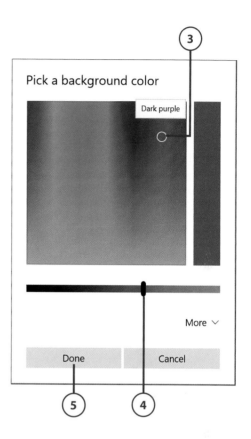

Pick a background color

Dark purple

More ∨

Done   Cancel

Adjusting Colors in Windows 10

If you'd like, Windows 10 can automatically pick out accent colors from the photos you select for the desktop background and then assign those colors to other elements of the user interface. You can also turn the feature off and, instead, manually assign colors to the Start menu, taskbar, and Windows 10 Action Center. You can control the transparency of the Start menu, taskbar, and Action Center. When you make the onscreen elements transparent, you can see the desktop image through them, for a nice effect.

Choosing Accent Colors and Transparency

Let Windows 10 know how you want the operating system to handle colors in the Colors category of the Personalization screen. You can choose which colors are used and determine whether you want the color to be displayed transparently in various onscreen elements.

1. Display the Personalization screen.

2. Click the Colors category.

3. To have Windows 10 automatically choose the accent color, leave the check box selected.

Choosing a Color

If you want to manually select a color scheme, including the colors used as accent colors on menus, the taskbar, and more, uncheck this check box.

4. Scroll down to see more options.

5. If you want to turn on the Transparency setting so you can see the desktop background through menus and pop-up windows, move the slider to On.

6. Choose whether you want the accent color to appear in the Start menu/screen, on the taskbar, and in Action Center.

7. Click to use the accent color on the title bars of app windows.

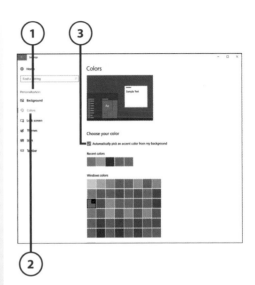

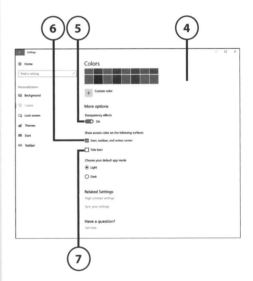

Enabling High Contrast and App Mode

Windows 10 includes a High Contrast option so that you can display Windows in a way that heightens the contrast on the screen. This option can be particularly helpful for colorblind users. You can find the High Contrast settings on the Colors page of the Personalization screen, and you can access them through the Ease of Access option in Settings.

You can choose whether you want to view your apps in Light or Dark mode. Changing the mode can enable you to better see the screen when you're working in variable light situations.

Begin by clicking Colors in the Personalization screen. Scroll down to the Related Settings area and click High Contrast Settings. Choose a theme from the Theme list and then click Apply. Windows 10 updates the display with the high-contrast theme you selected.

Setting a Night Light in Windows 10

Windows 10 Fall Creators Update offers a neat new feature that can cut down on the wear and tear on your eyeballs after dark. There is a blue quality in bright on-screen light that brings out the bright white in online displays. But when the light in the room grows dim, that blue adds a glaring quality that makes reading and viewing (and eventually, sleeping!) harder on our eyes. Recognizing this, the developers of Windows 10 Fall Creators Update added a new feature that automatically dims the light for you at night—or at a time you specify. The settings for Night Light are in the System settings.

1. Display the Settings window by clicking the Start button and choosing Settings.

2. Click System.

3. Click the Display category if it isn't already selected.

4. Drag the Night Light slider to the On position.

5. Click Night Light Settings to customize the time the setting goes into effect.

6. Drag the slider to adjust the color used at night.

7. Drag to the On position to schedule the Night Light hours.

8. Click to let Windows 10 set the Night Light schedule according to your local sunrise and sunset times.

9. Click to specify your own hours for Night Light.

10. Adjust the On and Off times for Night Light.

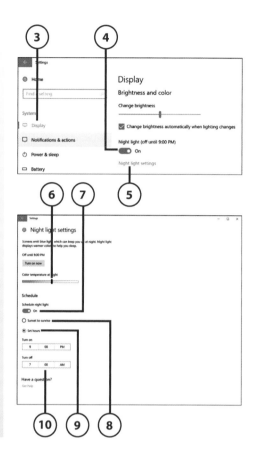

Personalizing the Lock Screen

The Lock screen is the first screen you see when you press Power and your Windows 10 PC or device comes to life. The Lock screen shows your profile image and also might show you some notifications—called badges—from your email, messaging, and calendar apps. For example, small numbers beside the notifications icons can show you how many email messages and instant messages you have. That's a great time-saver because you can see what needs your attention before you even unlock your computer!

You can also talk to Cortana without even unlocking your computer or device. You can simply say, "Hey, Cortana!" to wake it up and then speak your command. Pretty neat.

You can personalize the look of your Windows 10 Lock screen by changing your profile picture or by choosing your favorite Lock screen pictures. Windows 10 gives you a number of photos to choose from, but you can use one of your own personal images if you like. What's more, in Windows 10 you can create a custom slideshow using your favorite images from different sources, so the Lock screen displays family, friends, and more, even while your computer is locked.

Choosing a New Lock Screen Picture

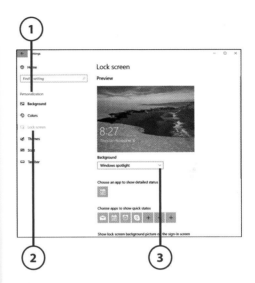

Initially, Windows 10 uses a default picture for your Lock screen, but you can change that image to show something that has personal meaning for you. You can change your Lock screen picture whenever you like by following these steps:

1. Display the Personalization settings.

2. Click the Lock Screen category.

3. From the Background list, select Picture.

Other Options

There are three options in this menu. Windows Spotlight displays images from Windows 10, Picture enables you to choose your own image for the lock screen, and Slideshow gives you the ability to create a slideshow of images from photos you select.

4. Click a photo if you want to use one that is shown in the thumbnail views.

5. Click Browse to select your own photo.

6. Click the folder containing the photo you want to use.

7. Click the photo you want to use.

8. Click Choose Picture to add the photo to the Lock screen.

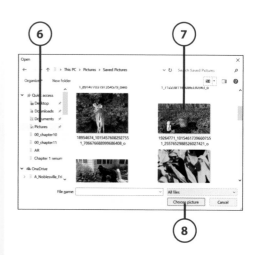

Adding a New Lock Screen Picture On-the-Fly

If you're viewing photos on your computer and see an image you particularly like, you can make that photo your Lock screen image instantly. Here's how to do that:

1. In the Photos app, display the photo you want to use as the Lock screen.

More Photo Tips, Please

You learn much more about working with photos in Windows 10 in Chapter 11, "Bringing Out Your Inner Artist with Photos and Paint 3D."

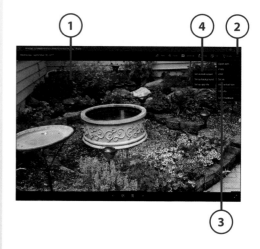

2. Click the three dots in the upper right to display the photo options list.

3. Click Set As.

Lock Screen Photos Quickly

You can use a shortcut key combination to choose a displayed photo as your Lock screen image. Display the photo using the Photos app and then press Ctrl+L.

---

4. Click Set as Lock Screen. The new photo is applied instantly as your Lock screen image.

Creating a Slideshow

Another feature in Windows 10 lets you create and play a slideshow on the Lock screen, which can add some ambiance to your room when you're not actively using your PC. Here's how to create a slideshow for your Lock screen:

1. Display the Lock Screen category in the Personalization screen.

2. Choose Slideshow from the Background list.

3. If you want Windows 10 to use photos from the Pictures folder on your PC or device, select Pictures.

4. If you want to choose a folder in another location (such as OneDrive folder), click Add a Folder and choose the folder you want to use.

5. Click Advanced Slideshow Settings to choose the way the pictures appear on your screen.

6. Choose whether you want to include only pictures that fit your screen.

7. Drag to On if you want the slideshow to include pictures stored in OneDrive and in your Camera Roll folder (while connected to your phone).

8. If you want to conserve battery power and turn off the slideshow when power is low, drag the slider to Off.

9. Click to choose when you want the slideshow to turn off (30 minutes, 1 hour, 3 hours, or Don't turn off).

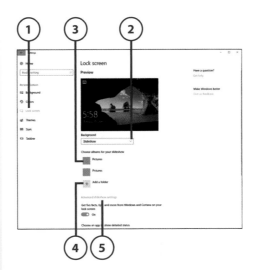

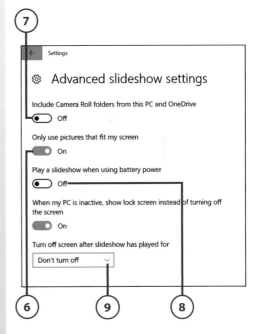

Stopping the Show

When you're ready to start working, you can tap, click, or press a key on the keyboard, and Windows 10 scrolls the slideshow away and displays your login information so you can enter your password or PIN and get to work.

>>>*Go Further*

CREATING THEMED SLIDESHOWS

You can easily create different slideshows for your Lock screen that suit your different moods or locations. For example, if you want to display a work-related slideshow during work hours (perhaps with photos of your latest projects or staff activities) and family images at home, you can store the different photos in folders named, appropriately, Work and Home; then you can choose the folder you want to use for the slideshow on-the-fly. This enables you to create as many slideshows as you like, and all you have to do is choose the folder with the images you want to show. Nice!

Choosing a Windows 10 Theme

It's a great thing to be able to change the colors, backgrounds, and more in Windows 10; that gives you control over the look of the operating system so you can work and play in an environment that suits you. One challenge, though, is that lots of personalizing could add up to a mish-mash of effects. Themes can help you fix that.

Windows 10 themes coordinate the look of your desktop background, color scheme, sounds, and screensaver. You can choose the theme in the Themes category of the Personalization screen.

Displaying Themes

1. Display the Personalization settings.

2. Choose Themes.

3. Click a Windows 10 theme you want to apply.

4. Change the background, color, sound, or mouse cursor settings to create a custom theme.

5. Click Save Theme to preserve the new changes.

6. Type a name for the theme.

7. Click Save to save the theme.

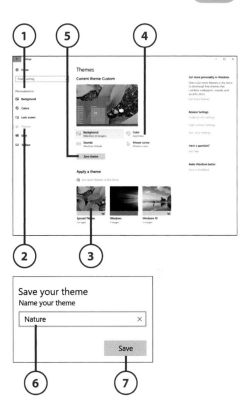

>>>Go Further

FINDING MORE THEME OPTIONS

If you don't see a theme that suits you, click the Get More Themes in the Store link. You'll find a variety of theme categories—new themes, animals, art, automotive, branded themes, games, holidays and seasons, movies, nature, and places and landscapes—to view a collection of themes related to the various topics. To find out more about a specific theme, click the theme tile. To download a theme you like, click the Get button. When the download is complete, a notification alerts you. You can click the notification to display the new theme. The new theme appears in the Apply a Theme section.

Customizing the Start Menu

By now you've probably used the Start menu a number of times, and you realize how easy it makes navigating to the settings and apps you need.

Although the Start menu is something of a return to the classic way of interacting with Windows, the Windows 10 Start menu goes several steps beyond what you may have been used to in Windows 7 or earlier versions. For example, the Windows 10 Start menu includes a Most Used list on the left and a grid of live tiles on the right that enable you to launch apps and access information faster than ever before.

You can customize the Start menu to adjust the list of programs that appear in the Most Recently Used list and even change the color of the Start menu if you like. You can also resize the Start menu by dragging it to the size you want and further personalize it by adding and arranging the app tiles you want to be able to access easily.

Give Me That Old-Time Start Menu

Here's a trick for the Windows 7 lovers among us. You can turn off the app tiles displayed on the right side of the Start menu. To do this, right-click each app tile and choose Unpin from Start. One by one, the app tiles go away, and soon, all you're left with is the Start menu Most Used list above the Start button. Who said there's no going back?

Modifying the Most Used List

The Most Used list at the top of the Start menu displays the program icons of the apps you've used most recently. You can change the programs displayed there by removing the ones you no longer need.

1. Click the Start button to display the Start menu.

2. Right-click the program icon of the item you want to remove in the Most Used list. A menu appears.

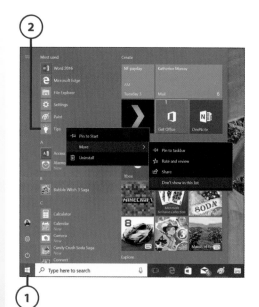

3. Click More. A submenu of choices appears.

Just Out of Sight, Not Gone Forever

When you remove a program from the most recently used list, you aren't doing anything to affect the program in any way. It is still installed in Windows 10, and you can find it by going to All Apps or clicking the Search tool and searching for the program name. If you meant to uninstall the program completely, you can do so by right-clicking the program in the list and choosing Uninstall from the menu that appears.

4. Click Don't Show in This List. The program icon and name is removed.

Is Your Most Used List Missing?

If you don't see a Most Used list at the top of your Start menu, it could be that the setting is turned off. To display the Most Used list, click Start, Settings, choose Personalization, and click Start. Verify that the Show Most Used Apps slider is set to On.

Changing Start Menu Settings

By modifying a few settings, you can change the way Windows 10 displays items on your Start menu. These settings are in the Start category of Settings. You can get to it by clicking Settings and then choosing Personalization, or you can use the shortcut shown in the following steps.

1. Right-click anywhere on the Windows 10 Desktop. A list of options appears.

2. Click Personalize. The Personalization settings appear.

3. Click the Start category.

4. To hide the display of the Most Used list in the Start menu, move this slider to Off.

On by Default

By default, most of the sliders shown here are set to On.

---

5. To turn off the display of recently added apps, drag this slider to the Off position.

6. If you want the Start menu to appear full-screen (similar to what you see in Tablet mode), move the slider to the On position.

7. By default, Windows 10 shows recently opened items in jump lists that appear on the taskbar and in the Start menu. To turn this off, drag the slider to Off.

8. Click Choose Which Folders Appear on Start to customize the folders displayed in the Start menu.

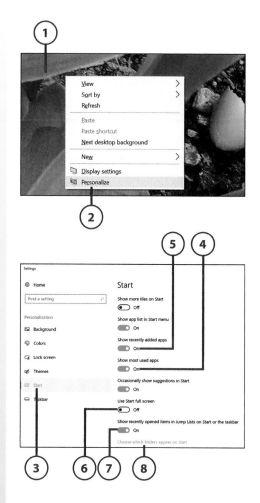

>>>*Go Further*

PIN THE RECYCLE BIN TO THE START MENU

If you use the Recycle Bin often and want to add it to the Start menu where you can reach it easily, right-click the Recycle Bin icon on your desktop, and choose Pin to Start.

The Recycle Bin is added as an app tile on your Start menu, where you can reach it as needed.

Resizing the Start Menu

By default, the Start menu stretches to half the width of your screen, if not more, showing lots of app tiles. You can resize the menu, if you like, so it takes up less or more space on your desktop.

1. Click the Start button to display the Start menu.

2. Hover the mouse over an edge of the menu. When it changes to a double-headed arrow, click and drag the border to the left or down.

3. To make the menu narrower, click the right border of the menu and drag to the left.

4. Drag the top border of the menu down to create a more compact effect.

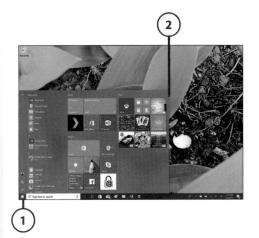

Tweaking Additional System Settings

Two more customizations you might want to make every so often include changing the time (especially if you're a traveler and don't have your computer set to adjust the time automatically) and the profile picture used with your Microsoft account. You can change both items right from your Windows 10 desktop.

Changing the Time

It's likely that the first time you log in to Windows 10, the program will ask you to verify or choose your time zone. By default, when connected to the Internet, Windows knows where you are and what time it is, allowing it to update your clock automatically. You can, however, manually set the time and time zone by following these steps:

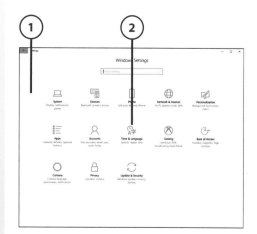

1. Select the Settings tool in the Start menu to open the Settings screen.

2. Click the Time & Language category.

3. If you want to adjust the time manually, turn Set Time Automatically to the Off position. The Change button becomes available.

4. Click the Change button and enter a new date and time.

5. Choose a new time zone by clicking the arrow and choosing your zone from the list.

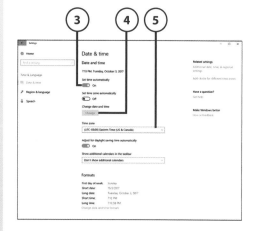

6. Leave the Adjust for Daylight Saving Time Automatically turned on if you want the time to be adjusted for you when Daylight Saving Time changes.

7. If you want to display your calendar in other languages (for example, Simplified Chinese), you can select the language from this list.

8. Click the link to change the format of the date and time if you want this information displayed differently.

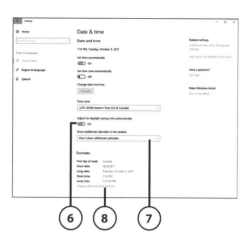

Changing Your Account Picture

Your account picture appears—in a tiny size—on the left side of your Windows Start menu. You also see it when you swipe up or click your Lock screen. You can change your account picture in Windows 10 as often as you like.

1. Display the Start menu.

2. Click your profile picture. A small menu appears.

3. Click Change Account Settings. The Accounts screen appears.

4. Click Browse for One to display the Open dialog box and choose a picture; click Choose Image to add the image.

5. If you want to add a picture using a camera connected to your computer, click Camera.

6. Your webcam display opens, showing a picture of you. When the picture you want to capture is displayed, tap or click anywhere on the screen to take the photo (not shown in figure).

Fewer Choices, Please

If you go through a whole slew of possible account picture choices and aren't particularly happy with any of them, you can remove the ones that appear as thumbnails beneath your chosen picture in the Account Picture screen. Right-click the picture and select Clear History. Windows wipes away the images you've added.

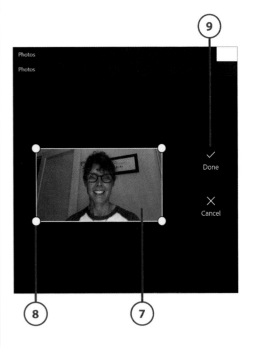

7. Windows 10 displays the picture in a preview screen.

8. Click the cropping handles to adjust what remains visible in the picture.

9. When the picture is displayed the way you want it to appear, tap or click Done.

Retaking a Photo

If you want to replace the photo you just captured, tap or click Retake and repeat steps 6 through 9. Windows 10 then substitutes the new photo for your Account Picture.

Windows Defender has been enhanced to provide significant new protections for your system.

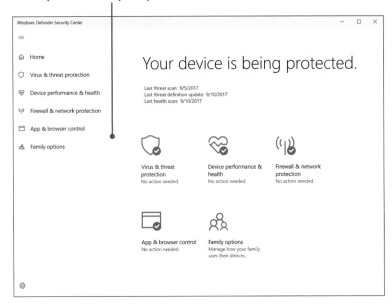

You can change location settings for individual apps to control who has access to your location information.

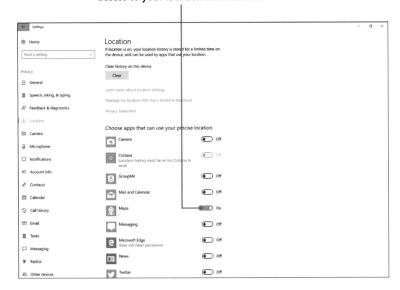

This chapter shows you how to keep your computer safe by focusing on the following tasks:

→ Customizing your login
→ Working with security and maintenance in Windows 10
→ Using Windows Defender
→ Working with user accounts
→ Maintaining your privacy

Securing Your Computer— for Yourself and Your Family

With Windows 10 Fall Creators Update, Microsoft has ramped up the attention given to making sure your computer is secure against online threats, identity theft, and more. We seem to live in an age of enormous data breaches, and the focus on security is well founded. Microsoft has previously done a good job of providing security features in Windows 10, but Fall Creators Update includes a substantial build-out for Windows Defender, the primary security app used by Windows 10, as well as new privacy tools so you can control how, when, and why your apps share information about your location and more.

In this chapter, we focus on the tools and techniques you can use in Windows 10 to make sure your computer is as secure as possible for you and your family. You learn how to create user accounts, assign permissions (including family safety features), and make sure you've got everything set up properly for a secure computing experience.

New PCs—Security *Before* Startup

In Windows 10, PCs that are built on Unified Extensible Firmware Interface (UEFI) firmware can take advantage of enhanced security features such as Secure Boot, which does a scan and ensures system elements are okay before Windows 10 even boots on your system. For most, just rest secure knowing you have this feature working for you, but if you'd like to learn more about UEFI, you should check out http://www.uefi.org.

Customizing Your Login

It seems like we're always logging in to one thing or another, doesn't it? We log in to our phones, our work computers, our home computers. Most of us want a smooth, simple login experience. Windows 10 offers a number of ways you can log in so that the process reflects what you find easiest to do. You might just log in with a simple four-digit pin or use a picture to draw a pattern on the screen that only you know.

It's Not All Good

SIMPLER ISN'T MORE SECURE

Although biometric security such as Windows Hello is generally more secure than passwords, the same cannot (necessarily) be said about picture passwords or PINs. Picture and PIN passwords can be more convenient, especially on touch-based devices, but that does not mean they're more secure. PIN passwords, in particular, are not more secure than a good alphanumeric password.

New security features in Windows 10 also include Windows Hello, which uses facial recognition and iris scans to authenticate users and ensure the computer's security. These new technologies require infrared cameras on Windows 10 devices, so the practical use of these features might be a little further into the future. Windows Hello also supports existing fingerprint readers, which may be included on laptops or tablets or used as plug-in devices via USB.

>>>Go Further
FINDING WINDOWS HELLO

You might be surprised to see that in your Windows Hello settings on the Sign-In Options screen, there's a big smiley face but no way to set up the feature. No options. Nothing to add. You might see a note that says, "Windows Hello isn't available on this device."

This happens because Windows 10 displays the Set Up buttons for Fingerprint and Face features only if your computer is equipped with a fingerprint reader or an infrared camera that gives your system the facial recognition capabilities it needs in order to use Windows Hello.

If you add a fingerprint reader or an infrared camera at a later point, come back to Windows Hello, and you'll see that those options are now available.

Changing a Password

By default, Windows 10 prompts you to log in with your Microsoft account and password. You can, however, change your password at any time or choose different types of passwords (for example, a picture password or a PIN logon) to help with authentication.

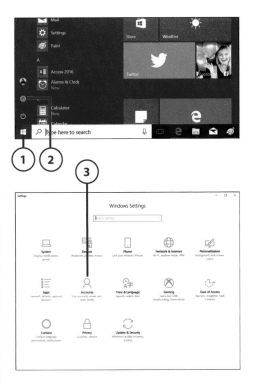

1. Click the Start button to display the Start menu.

2. Select Settings.

3. Choose Accounts in the Settings window.

4. Click Sign-In Options.

Change Password Type

On the right side of the screen, you may see up to four ways to make changes for your Sign-In Options: Password, PIN, Windows Hello, and Picture Password. I cover these other options in the following tasks. (Note that Windows Hello is available only if your system has the capabilities that support the technology for those features.)

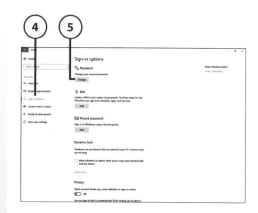

5. In the Password area, click Change. You're prompted to enter your Microsoft Account password. After you enter it, the Change Password screen appears.

6. In the Change Your Password screen, type your old password in the Old Password box.

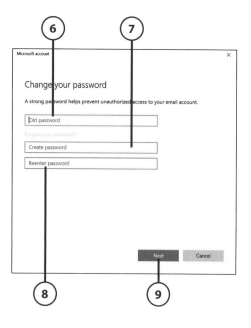

Local Accounts

If you use a Local Windows account instead of a Microsoft account, this screen will look a bit different, but the basic procedure remains the same.

7. Click to move the insertion point to the Create Password box, and enter a new password.

8. Retype the new password in the Reenter Password box.

9. Click Next. Windows 10 lets you know that you've successfully changed your password, and you can click Finish to return to the Accounts window.

But First...

If this is the first time you've changed your password on your Windows 10 computer, the operating system may prompt you with a few security measures before allowing you to change it. You might see a message that asks you to confirm your secondary email address and then enter a code Microsoft sends to that account to ensure your account security. Once you enter the code and click Next, you see the Change Password screen so you can make the change you want.

Account Trouble?

If you have forgotten the password you used with your Microsoft Account, you can still change your password online. Click the Forgot Your Password? link where you enter your login information, and Windows 10 displays a link you can click to go online to resolve the problem.

>>>Go Further
SETTING STRONG PASSWORDS

A strong password is at least eight characters long and doesn't include recognizable words or number sequences. What's more, you should vary the capitalization of letters, mixing the upper- and lowercase letters. Windows 10 remembers your password as case sensitive, which means that 62GoT38 is a different password from 62gOt38.

Creating a PIN Logon

Chances are you're familiar with using PINs in other areas of your life. You use a PIN for your debit card, and you might have one set on your smartphone, for example. Similarly, Windows 10 enables you to create a four-digit PIN to use when you log in to your computer or device.

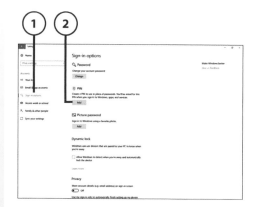

1. Click Sign-In Options in the Accounts section of Settings.

2. In the PIN area, click Add. Windows 10 prompts you to enter your current password. After you do so, the Set Up a Pin screen appears.

3. Type the four numbers you want to use as your PIN.

4. Click in the Confirm PIN box and retype the numbers you entered.

5. If you want to use numbers, letters, and symbols in your PIN, click the Include Letters and Symbols checkbox. A PIN Requirements link will appear to give you guidelines on how to create an effective PIN.

6. Click or tap OK. Windows 10 saves your PIN; the next time you log in, you can enter the PIN instead of your password. Windows displays the Start screen immediately, even before you press Enter!

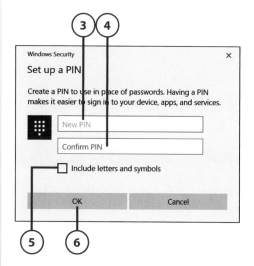

Nothing Fancy, Bub

When you create a PIN, Windows 10 insists you use only numbers—and only four of those, if you click the Use a 4-Digit PIN check box when you set up your PIN. This means no alphabetic characters, punctuation symbols, or spaces. This is less secure than a strong alphanumeric password.

Removing a PIN

If you decide you want to remove your PIN later, you can display the Sign-In Options tab of the Accounts screen again and in the PIN area click Remove. You can also change the PIN you created by clicking Change and entering and saving a new PIN.

Creating a Picture Password

Here are the steps to add a picture password:

1. Display the Accounts window in Settings, and click Sign-In Options.

2. In the Picture Password area, tap or click Add. Select Create a Picture Password. Windows prompts you to enter your current password. Type it and click OK.

Is It Really You?

Before you can create the picture password, Windows 10 prompts you to enter your password to confirm that it is authentically you wanting to change the password style.

---

3. The Welcome to Picture Password window appears, giving you instructions about the process of creating a picture password. Click Choose Picture. The Open window appears.

4. Locate and select the picture you want to use.

5. Click Open.

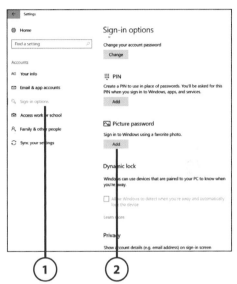

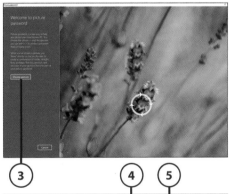

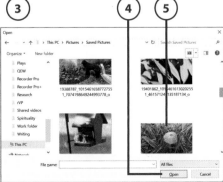

6. If you want to adjust the picture, drag it to the right or left, up or down.

7. Click Use This Picture.

Change the Picture

If you want to choose a different image instead, click Choose New Picture and repeat steps 4 through 7.

8. Using your finger or mouse, draw three gestures on the picture. For a moment after you draw on the screen, an arrow shows how Windows recorded the movement. When prompted, repeat the gestures. If you don't make exactly the same gestures, Windows prompts you to try again.

Starting Over

If you don't like the gesture you've used, you can tap or click Start Over to create new gestures.

9. After you draw the gestures correctly, Windows displays a Congratulations message. Click Finish to save the picture password.

Don't Worry, Be Happy

Don't panic if you forget your picture password. Windows 10 can help you. Go to the Sign-In Options page of the Accounts window and tap the Change button in the Picture Password area. In the next window, after you enter your Microsoft Account password, you can click Replay to see a repeat of the gestures you used to create your password. You can also create a new picture password if you prefer.

Removing a Picture Password

If you want to remove your picture password, display the Sign-In Options screen of the Accounts window. Click the Remove button that now appears to the right of the Change button in the Picture Password area to delete the picture password you added.

It's Not All Good

THE FUSSINESS OF PICTURE PASSWORDS

One thing you're likely to discover quickly: Picture passwords are very particular. Windows 10 might not record your gesture exactly as you think you entered it. If you draw an arc on the screen, Windows might close it to create a circle. Or the line you purposely skewed might show up straight. Use the Try Again option to display the gestures Windows 10 is expecting.

It can also help to use a photo that has very definite patterns or lines you can follow and remember easily. Too many curves or too much abstraction can leave you wondering about the specific gestures you need to enter. On the other hand, following an image's precise curves or features is easier for someone else to guess. Pick your poison.

For Bluetooth Machines: Dynamic Lock

If your PC or tablet has Bluetooth capabilities, you can rely on Windows Hello to lock your device for you automatically when you walk out of Bluetooth range. To set things up, begin by turning on Bluetooth and pairing your PC and phone so they are connected.

To turn on Dynamic Lock on your Windows 10 computer, display the Sign In Options window, and click the Allow Windows to Detect When You're Away and Automatically Lock the Device check box. Now anytime you pick up your phone and walk away, as soon as you get out of Bluetooth range, Windows 10 automatically locks your computer. Pretty slick, eh?

Working with Security and Maintenance in Windows 10

In previous versions of Windows, Microsoft included the Action Center as a kind of hub for your system security. You would get a notification from the

Action Center, for example, when something important related to your system's safety came up. This might be something such as a pop-up message telling you that you're running out of backup space on your hard drive or your antivirus program needs an update.

With Windows 10, Microsoft took a different approach with the Action Center. Now the center has become a hub of notifications of all sorts, which includes social media updates and new email notices, as well as messages from your computer or device that need your attention. For a quick look at the notifications, you can click the Notifications icon in the status tray of the taskbar or swipe in from the right edge of the screen. To get to the tools you need to make sure your system is working well, open the Security and Maintenance window.

Reviewing Your System Status

You can easily see which security tools are in place on your computer, change settings, and update your software in the Security and Maintenance window of the Control Panel. Here's how to get there:

1. Click in the Search box in the taskbar, and type **security and maintenance**.

2. Click Security and Maintenance.

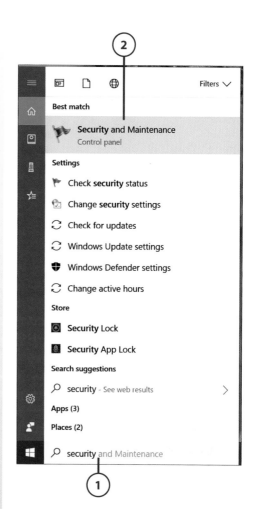

3. Click the arrow to the right of the Security or Maintenance categories to display details about the tools in each of those areas

4. In the Security and Maintenance window, review any messages that are displayed.

5. Click the link that is provided for any tools you want to review or change settings for.

6. Click the arrow to close the expanded tool list when you're finished reviewing.

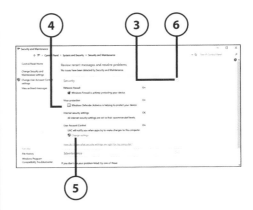

Not Sure What You Need?

If you aren't clear about what types of security measures you should have in place, you can let Microsoft help you make the call. Expand the Security list in the Security and Maintenance window, and scroll down to the bottom of the list. Click the How Do I Know What Security Settings Are Right for My Computer? link; Windows Help and Support displays the Security Checklist for Windows so you can learn about the different tools and make changes as needed.

>>>Go Further

WHY WORRY ABOUT USER ACCOUNT CONTROL?

It's not unusual today when you're downloading files from the Web to encounter websites and online programs that want to make changes to your computer. Some of these files are legitimate—perhaps you need the latest version of Microsoft Silverlight or Adobe Flash to play a movie trailer. But some programs are not so well intentioned, and these are the ones you need User Account Control to block.

User Account Control lets you easily find out when a program wants to make a change to your computer. You can set up User Account Control so you'll be notified when a program tries to change your system settings. (It's set to do this by default.) Windows 10 offers four settings, ranging from Always Notify to Never Notify, and you can easily change the settings by clicking Change User Account Control Settings in the left panel of the Control Panel. Although User Account Control prompts can be annoying, before you disable them, remember that they're there for your protection.

Changing Security and Maintenance Alerts

Each Security and Maintenance message includes a link that gives you the next step to follow as you deal with the issue. You can choose to turn off messages about that particular issue, archive the message, or ignore the message. You can change which issues you receive alerts for so that you are notified about only the ones you want to see.

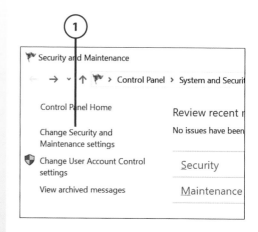

1. In the Security and Maintenance window, click Change Security and Maintenance Settings.

2. Click to uncheck any security item you don't want Windows 10 to check for.

Choice—It's Your Prerogative

You can change the items Windows 10 checks for and the messages you receive at any time. If you turn off an item and then get concerned that maybe you need it after all, go to the Security and Maintenance window, click Change Security and Maintenance Settings again, and click to check any unmarked boxes of items you want to add. Click OK to save your settings.

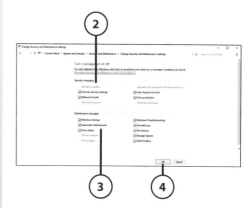

3. Click to uncheck any maintenance messages you don't want Windows 10 to display.

4. Click OK.

Out of Sight, Out of Mind

Although being alerted for every little thing can be annoying, unless you have a specific reason for turning off an alert—for example, Windows 10 doesn't recognize the antivirus program you're using and keeps telling you there's no antivirus program installed—the best practice is to leave all the alerts turned on.

Using Windows Defender

Windows Defender has gotten a big boost in Windows 10 Fall Creators Update. Now the app, which was formerly an anti-spyware utility designed to protect your computer from spyware and other intrusions, has grown up into a multifaceted protection system that keeps an eye on the health of your computer, scans regularly for viruses and malware, intercepts unrecognized apps, safeguards your system with Windows Firewall, and enables you to set up family security options so you know protection is in place for everyone in your household who uses your computer.

If you're concerned that your computer is infected, you can use Windows Defender to scan your system regularly and remove any suspicious files that have been added to your computer without your knowledge. Windows Defender in Windows 10 also includes a network monitoring feature that helps computers on a network detect and stop malware.

It's Not All Good

CAN'T WE ALL JUST GET ALONG?

One of the challenges of working with antivirus, spyware, and malware protection programs is that they don't play nicely together. As you can imagine, they are suspicious of everyone; that's their job.

This means that if you have installed another type of antivirus or spyware program, such as Lavasoft's Ad-Aware or Norton 360, Windows Defender might be disabled.

If you'd rather have Windows Defender operating, you might need to uninstall the other antivirus or spyware software before you can activate Windows Defender. This can be a pain, but if you've deliberately paid for and installed a different security suite, chances are it means you trust it to do a more thorough job than Microsoft's solution. And Windows Defender Security—especially in its enhanced form, for Windows 10 Fall Creators Update—is built to work with your operating system, so it is likely to be a solid choice for protection.

Checking Out the Windows Defender Security Center

Windows Defender is always working in the background of your Windows 10 computer or device, but you can check the status of the scans, tweak settings, and more by displaying the Windows Defender Security Center.

1. Type **defender** into the Search box in the taskbar. The Search pane appears, showing Windows Defender in the results.

2. Click Windows Defender Security Center.

3. Notice when the last scan of your system was performed.

4. Review the status of the various security tools. Windows 10 lets you know if any action is needed from you at this time.

5. Click one of the security categories to see updates related to those areas.

6. Click Settings to change the way in which Windows Defender notifies you of issues and updates.

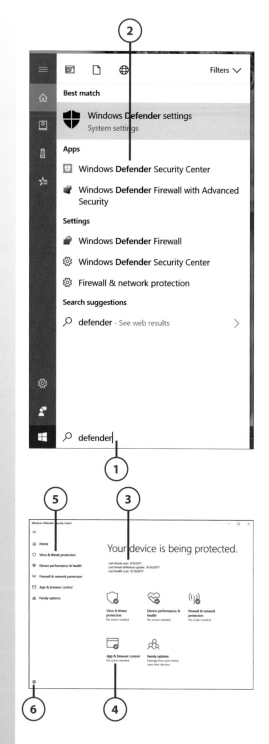

Scanning for Risks with Windows Defender

Windows Defender is designed to scan your system every so often—at increments you choose—but you can also choose to do a scan of your PC whenever you like.

You can launch Windows Defender from the Settings window, or you can launch Defender as an app from the Start menu. Either way, you can have Windows Defender scan your PC to make sure no worrisome files have snuck in under your radar.

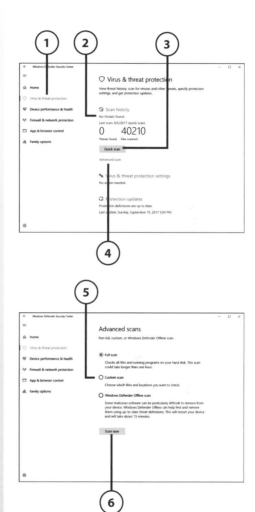

1. In the Windows Defender Security Center, click Virus & Threat Protection.

2. Review the information about the most recent scan.

3. To launch a new scan, click the Quick Scan button. Windows Defender immediately begins scanning your computer or device.

4. If you want to do an in-depth scan, click Advanced Scan.

5. Choose the option you want for the type of scan you want Windows Defender to perform. You can do a Quick scan, a Full scan, or a Custom scan.

6. Tap or click the Scan Now button. Windows Defender begins the scanning process.

Choose a Scan

If you have specific concerns about a security threat, choose a Full scan. It takes longer, but it is more thorough in scanning all your computer's files.

Updating Your Definitions

Windows Defender uses what's known as a definitions file to make sure it's checking for the latest viruses and spyware. Defender automatically updates the file, but you can also have Defender check to see whether any new updates are available. Click the Virus & Threat Protection category and choose Protection Updates. Then tap or click the Check for Updates button to search for updates to the definitions file.

7. After the scan completes, Windows Defender updates the scan information in the Virus & Threat Protection category and sends a system notification alerting you that the scan is complete.

A Quick System Checkup

We talk more about the overall health of your computer, and how to keep your version of Windows 10 up to date, in Chapter 14, "Caring for Your Computer and Updating Windows." Just make a mental note that the Device Performance & Health category in Windows Defender keeps an eye on such things for you. You can get a quick check on update issues, storage space, driver updates, and battery life in this area of Windows Defender.

Defender shows the results of the scan.

The app lets you know the scan is complete.

Checking Your Windows Firewall

A firewall checks all the information coming to your computer from the Internet or any local network to which you are connected. Firewalls try to ensure that any data received comes from a trusted contact and that the information can be considered safe for your computer. If any suspicious information is found, your Windows Firewall alerts you so that you can allow or block the sender based on whether you think it should be allowed through the firewall. Windows Firewall used to be a standalone tool that functioned in the protection of your system, but in Windows 10 Fall Creators Update, Windows Firewall has been integrated into Windows Defender Security.

Checking the Firewall

Windows Defender keeps your Firewall on by default. You can, however, check the settings and turn the utility off or on again if necessary.

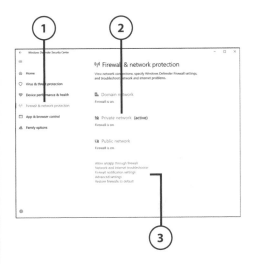

1. In the Windows Defender Security Center, click the Firewall & Network Protection category.

2. Review the status of the firewalls used on your system. The green check mark means the firewall is on and functioning properly.

3. Click a setting to make changes to it.

How Many Firewalls Do I Need?

You are likely to see three different firewall settings: domain, private, and public When you are working on your home network, you typically are using a private network. When you are using your computer or device in a public place, like a library or coffee shop, the public firewall is used. And if you log in to a workplace network, you might be using the domain firewall. It's important that each of these firewalls be in place so that Windows Defender can keep an eye on the overall protection of your system.

Changing Firewall Settings

When Windows Firewall is active, you are prompted each time a program tries to make changes on your computer that don't appear to come from an authorized source. You can change the settings for Windows Firewall so that you receive different alerts using different criteria if you like.

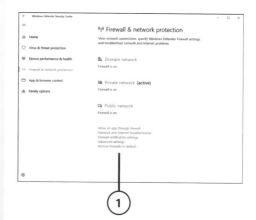

1. In the bottom area of the Firewall & Network Protection window, click Firewall Notification Settings.

2. Leave this setting set to On if you want to continue receiving notifications of all Defender activity and scan results.

3. Leave this set to On if you want to know when Windows Defender blocks a suspicious app.

4. If you want to stop notifications for one of the different network areas (for example, for the domain firewall), click to clear the check mark in the check box.

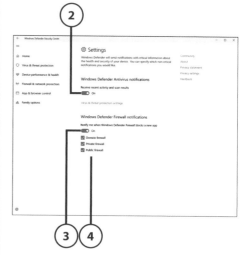

Public Security

Public networks are generally more unsecure than private home or office networks. Windows Firewall is more stringent in what it treats as trustworthy over a public network.

Working with Windows SmartScreen

Windows SmartScreen is another Windows 10 utility that used to be a standalone app and is now included as part of Windows Defender Security Center. Windows SmartScreen keeps an eye on your computer or device and alerts you before Windows 10 runs any unrecognized apps or files you've downloaded from the Web.

By default, Windows SmartScreen displays a warning before running an unrecognized app. You can change Windows SmartScreen settings if you want to, either to turn off the feature (not a good idea) or to require that administrator approval be given before an unrecognized app can be run.

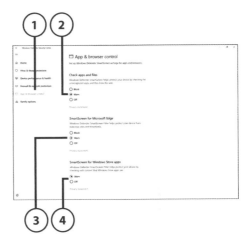

1. In the Windows Defender Security Center, click App & Browser Control. The window shows a number of settings from Windows SmartScreen designed to help safeguard your computer from unwanted apps. Each of the settings is set to warn you of any suspicious files or apps.

2. Choose whether you want to be warned about apps and files, whether you want to block them entirely, or whether you want to turn SmartScreen off (not recommended).

3. Choose whether to block or be warned about malicious sites and potentially dangerous downloads while you're using the Edge browser.

4. Choose to protect your computer by checking the web content that various Microsoft Store apps might use.

Setting Up Family Options

Now Windows Defender Security Center also includes a category for setting up security and protection for your family members. The settings are tied to the user accounts for your kids, so you can set age-appropriate controls and even set up schedules for web surfing and gameplay.

In the Windows Defender Security Center, click Family Options, and click View Family Settings. This takes you to a site online connected to your Microsoft Account, where you can make choices about reviewing the computer activity of your children, choose whether to block certain types of websites, limit the types of games your kids have access to, and create a schedule that manages the amount of time and the time of day your kids can use the computer.

Working with User Accounts

User accounts have been around for a while, and if you share a computer with several people in your household, you know they are a good idea. When you have separate accounts for different users, you can each have your own preferences and favorite websites and programs. This makes it possible for each of you to have a completely different experience—tailored to your own preferences—even though you're all sharing the same computer.

Adding a User

Individual users can have their own user account so that specific preferences, histories, favorites, and more can be linked with that account. It's a good idea to create separate user accounts for each person who shares your computer or device. Windows 10 enables you to add two kinds of users: a family member or a user who isn't a family member.

1. Type **account** into the Search box in the taskbar.

2. Click Add, Edit, or Remove Other People in the results list.

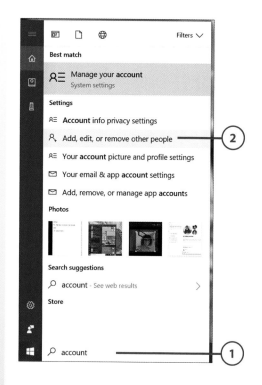

3. Tap or click the + to the left of Add a Family Member.

Other Users

Select Add Someone Else to This PC if the account you want to add is not a family member or regular user. The steps for adding these users is similar to what you see here, except there is no child/adult selection.

4. The Add a User window appears, asking you whether the new family member is an adult or a child. Click your answer.

5. Enter the person's email address.

6. Click Next.

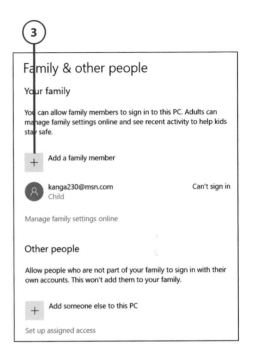

7. Click Confirm. Windows 10 tells you to make sure the person knows he needs to be connected to the Internet the first time he logs in.

Child Accounts

If the account you're creating is for a child, you see Family Safety options on this screen. Click the check box beneath the new user's profile picture placeholder to turn on Family Safety settings.

>>>Go Further

AN ACCOUNT BY ANY OTHER NAME

When you add a new user, you'll have the choice to sign the person up using her Microsoft Account or sign up with a Local Account specific to that computer. The difference is that when a person signs in using a Microsoft account, all system preferences—including notification settings, color schemes, and more—are available.

Using a Microsoft account also enables users to download apps from the Microsoft Store and save content to the cloud using OneDrive. If the new user doesn't sign in with a Microsoft account, settings and preferences are stored on the local machine.

Switching Users

You can easily switch among the user accounts on your Windows 10 computer by clicking or tapping your profile icon on the left side of the Start menu. You also can sign out of Windows 10, lock your computer, or change users.

1. Open the Start menu.

2. Click or tap the profile area (either your username or your picture) on the left side of the Start menu.

Switching on a Touchable

If you're using the Start screen on a touch device, your profile icon is located in the lower-left corner of the Start screen. Tap your profile picture to display the options for logging out and changing accounts.

3. Tap or click Lock to display your Lock screen and safeguard your computer. You might choose this when leaving your computer unattended for a while.

4. Tap or click Sign Out when you want to sign out of Windows 10, perhaps so that another user can log in.

5. Tap or click another user account to display the login screen for that account. The other user can enter the account password and click Submit to log in.

On Logging Out

If you log out of Windows 10, the next time you dismiss the Lock screen by swiping the touchscreen or pressing any key, all user accounts on your computer appear on the next screen so that you can tap or click the one you want to use to log in. You can then enter the password that goes along with that account to sign in to Windows 10.

Maintaining Your Privacy

Windows 10 makes it simple for you to share information among apps, both online and off. Your apps can use your location data to set your time zone, display the weather, offer location-related search results, and much more.

On the flip side of all this sharing are two important questions: How do these apps share this information, and how much data do you really want to turn loose out there in cyberspace? Windows 10 lets you determine whether you want your apps to communicate with each other and share information about you—such as your location or content URLs from the apps you use—with others who are interested in gathering it.

Turn Off Location for Your Kids

Location settings are of special concern to parents who are doing their best to safeguard their kids online. Although teens know for the most part they shouldn't share personal information on social media sites, some sites publish location information if those settings are turned on. If you have a child using social media, make sure location is turned off on phones and computing devices.

Choosing Privacy Settings

To review and modify privacy settings, follow these steps:

1. Type **privacy** into the Search box on the taskbar.

2. Click Privacy Settings.

3. To allow Windows 10 to share your search information so ads are more targeted to your interests, leave this set to the On position.

4. Leave this set to On if you want web content to be personalized to your local area using your languages list.

5. Leave this set to On if you want to let Windows notice which apps you open often to improve the Start menu and search results.

6. Leave this setting On if you want to receive suggestions in the Settings app.

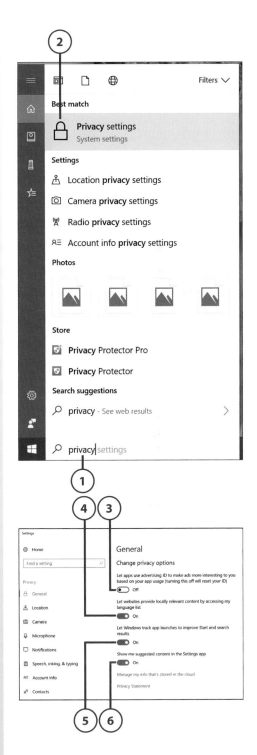

>>>Go Further

WHAT'S IN A PRIVACY STATEMENT?

When you click the Privacy Statement link on the Privacy screen, you are taken online to the Windows page where the statement is posted. This statement explains what personal information is gathered, what your choices are, and how the information is used.

Setting Location Privacy

Here's how to change your location settings:

1. Display Settings and choose Privacy.

2. Click Location.

3. If you want to turn location settings completely off, click the Change button. A small pop-up box appears. Drag the Location slider to the Off position.

4. Scroll down through the window until you can see the location settings for your apps.

5. If you want to leave location settings on but allow only selected apps to use them, go through your apps list and slide all those you do not want to have access to your location to the Off position.

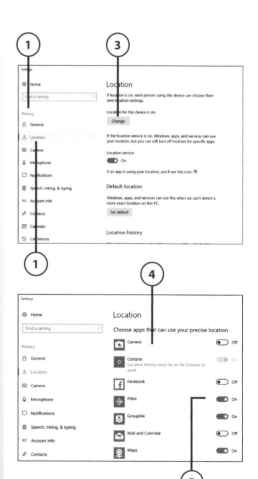

It's Not All Good

RISKY BUSINESS

Although giving apps access to your location can have benefits (finding local restaurants, showing friends on Facebook where you are so they can join you, and so on), it also brings concerns. First, with our ongoing struggle between privacy and security, we don't always want to be on other peoples' radar screens. Second, some people can use that information in ways that could pose a risk. For example, you don't want potential predators to be able to know where in the city your child is posting from or provide too much information about your location if you are going to be away.

You can scroll through
apps listed alphabetically
in the Start menu.

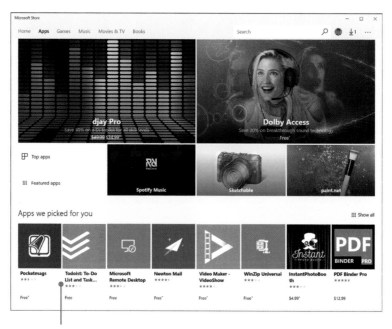

You can review, purchase,
download, and install apps
easily in Microsoft Store.

This chapter shows you how to use and update apps in Windows 10 by teaching these tasks:

→ Getting started with apps
→ Finding and starting apps
→ Moving, grouping, and removing apps
→ Working with apps
→ Closing apps
→ Getting apps from the Microsoft Store

Discovering, Using, and Sharing Favorite Apps

From the moment you first power up your Windows 10 computer or device, you'll notice that the operating system comes with a number of apps you can use. As your experience with Windows 10 grows, you'll no doubt add more and more apps that fit the way you work and the type of entertainment and activity (such as games) you enjoy in your free time. You can find thousands of apps in all sorts of categories in the Microsoft Store.

Because Microsoft's ultimate goal is a unified interface that works seamlessly across all kinds of computers and devices, the apps in the Microsoft Store are known as universal apps that are designed to work consistently across all types of computing formats. For example, the Netflix app is a universal app, available in desktop, tablet, Xbox, and phone versions, all of which work similarly so you know what you're doing no matter which technology you're using. Microsoft says that for universal apps, the code behind the scenes is 80 percent the same from device to device—there's only a 20 percent difference involved in fitting the app for the phone, your tablet, or your Xbox.

This chapter introduces you to working with the apps on your computer or device and shows you how to find, download, and update apps from the Microsoft Store.

Getting Started with Apps

Windows 10 includes a number of apps you can use as soon as you fire up the operating system. You'll find what you need to check and send email, set appointments on your calendar, connect with others through messaging, catch up on the latest in your favorite social media accounts, and open Microsoft Edge for some mindless browsing. These apps give you a good start on the types of tasks you want to accomplish in Windows 10, but this is only the beginning. You can download literally thousands of apps from the Microsoft Store, and developers are posting new apps there all the time.

The Windows 10 Start menu does a good job of giving you access to all the apps installed on your computer or tablet. On the right side of the menu, you see app tiles, which provide bits of information like what the weather looks like today, how many unread emails you have, or what the latest headlines are. On the left side of the menu, you see the apps you've used most recently, and you can scroll through an alphabetical list of your installed apps to find the one you want.

Starting in Tablet Mode

As you learned in an earlier chapter, Windows 10 Creators Update is designed to anticipate what kind of computer or device you're using and start up in the mode that is right for your hardware. If you're using a tablet, Windows 10 launches in Tablet mode, which means the Start menu looks like a grid of app tiles that stretches across the screen. To see the alphabetical list of all apps on your tablet, tap the All Apps tool in the upper left of the Start screen.

Checking Out Your Apps on the Start Menu

The Start menu actually does a good job of organizing many different apps into one relatively small, easy-to-access space. When you click or tap the Start button, you can choose apps in the following ways:

1. Click or tap a recently added app.

2. Choose an app from the Most Used list.

3. Tap or click the name of an app in the alphabetical list. (Scroll down to see more.)

4. Click or tap the app tile for the app you want to open.

5. Click or tap an app icon in the taskbar.

Pinning Apps to the Start Menu and the Taskbar

As you look through all the apps on the Start menu, you might discover a few you'd like to add to the app tiles on the right side of the menu. You can also add apps you use often to the taskbar at the bottom of the screen. You can pin new apps easily—and unpin apps you no longer need—by following these steps:

1. Click the Windows Start button to display the Start menu.

2. Scroll through the app list if necessary to locate the app you want to use, and then right-click it.

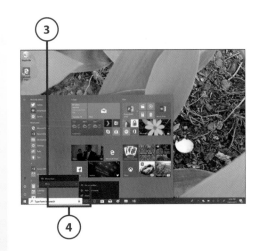

3. Click Pin to Start if you want the app to be added as a tile to the app grid in the Start menu.

4. Alternatively, click More and click Pin to Taskbar to add the app to the taskbar at the bottom of the screen.

Moving Apps Around

You can easily move an app tile to any point on your Start menu by tapping and holding, or clicking and dragging, it to a new location. The other apps in the destination area move to make room for the new app. You'll learn more about this later in this chapter.

Finding and Starting Apps

When you have dozens—or even hundreds—of apps installed on your computer or device, finding the specific one you want can be difficult. Luckily, you can use the Windows 10 Search box to quickly locate the app you're looking for.

Finding an App

The Search box in the taskbar has a dual purpose; it calls Cortana to your aid in finding information, events, and activities you're looking for. You can also use Search as a traditional Search tool, and it is a powerful one. Search quickly does a comprehensive search of your computer or device—including online storage—and produces a results list that shows apps, settings, files, and more. Here's how to use it to find the app you want:

1. Click in the Search box on the taskbar.

2. Type the name of the app you'd like to find.

3. Click or tap the app name in the results list that reflects the app you want to launch.

Downloading and Installing, Too

You'll learn more about what to do with the apps after you've found them, if they aren't already installed on your computer or device, later in this chapter.

Launching an App from the Start Menu

Microsoft gives you a couple of options for launching apps from the Start menu. You can click the link in the list on the left or click the tile that represents the program you want to run. As you learned earlier, you can also launch an app you've pinned to the taskbar.

1. Click the Start button to display the Start menu.

2. Click the program you want to launch.

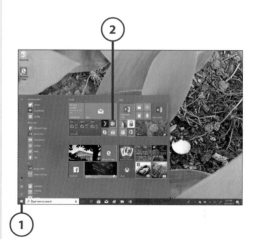

Moving, Grouping, and Removing Apps

You can organize the apps available on the Start menu so that you can find them easily. This could involve moving apps around on the menu, grouping them in ways that make sense to you, or removing ones you don't need. If you remove an app from the Windows 10 Start menu, you aren't removing it from your computer altogether; you are simply taking it off the menu.

Moving Apps on the Start Screen

You can rearrange the apps on the Start menu to better fit the way you work.

1. Select the app you want to move by clicking and holding it.

2. Drag the app tile to the new location. When you release the app tile, the other app tiles are rearranged to make room for the new app tile position.

Cleaning Up

One of my pet peeves is having wide and square tiles arranged on top of each other, resulting in blank space in the columns. So, I rearrange things to make the best use of space. The nice thing in Windows 10 is that you can put them in any order you like.

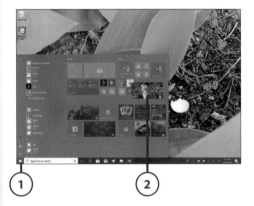

Creating an App Group

Notice that the Windows 10 Start menu includes a couple of "islands" of app tiles, with some grouped together with a little space between groups. You can change the way the groups are organized by moving app tiles from one group to another or by creating your own groups.

1. Click and hold the tile you want to move.

2. Drag it to the space between one of the app groups on the Start menu, and release the tile. A horizontal bar appears to show you where the tile will be placed when you release it.

3. Grab other apps, drag them to the same space, and release them. Windows adds space around the group so that you can see it easily as a group.

Making It All Fit

You can easily resize the app tiles after you add them to the new group by selecting the app tile and choosing Resize in the Apps bar. Then select the size you want the tile to be. Windows 10 rearranges the tiles in the group for you.

Naming App Groups

After you've created your app groups, you can further organize them by assigning a group name that appears on the Start screen. You can give your groups any name you like and change the name as often as it suits you.

1. On the Start menu, click in the blank area above the app group. A text box opens.

2. Type a name for the group.

3. Click outside the text box (or press Enter). The name appears above the group you selected.

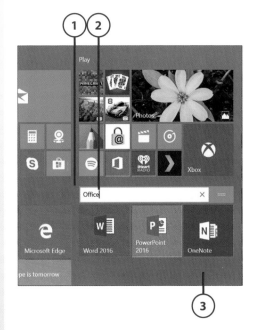

Removing an App from the Start Menu

If you want to remove some of the unnecessary apps that appear on the Start menu by default, you can do that easily and give yourself a little extra room.

1. Click the Start button to display the Start menu.

2. Right-click the app tile you want to remove. A list of app options appears.

3. Click Unpin from Start to unpin the app so that it is still installed on your computer but not visible as an app on the Start menu.

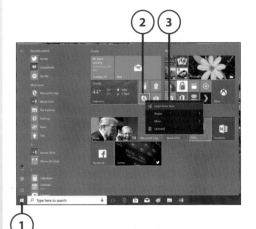

Working with Apps

In early versions of Windows, the "windows" in which your programs appeared were decidedly pronounced. You could always see the window frame—including the title bar, the Close box, the scrollbars, and the status bar at the bottom—no matter what task you might be performing. With Windows 8 came the advent of "modeless" or "windowless" windows. The idea is to create a more transparent computing experience so you aren't quite so aware of the periphery of what you're doing and you can focus wholeheartedly on your work inside the window.

In Windows 10, you see modeless windows only if you're using Tablet mode. In that mode, being able to use the entire width and breadth of the screen becomes important. You can swipe in to display the window border, but by default, you see borderless windows on your tablet.

On the desktop, however, you see the familiar window borders, complete with title bar, Quick Launch toolbar, Close box, status bar, and more.

>>>Go Further
SWITCHING AMONG OPEN APPS

Similar to the way you moved from one app to another in previous versions of Windows, you can see your open apps by pressing Alt+Tab in Windows 10. Now, however, the key combination displays Task view, showing thumbnail images of your open apps. Each time you press Tab while holding Alt, Windows 10 moves to the next open app on your computer. Release the keys when the app you want to use is highlighted.

You can also click the Task View tool, available in the taskbar, to display a more static version of Alt+Tab. Clicking the Task View tool displays all open apps on the screen at once so that you can click the one you want to use next.

Exploring an App Window

Depending on whether you open an app in Desktop mode or Tablet mode, the app might appear in the Windows 10 modeless style or in the more traditional desktop style. Here's a quick look at some common features of app windows:

- **Title bar**—The title bar of the window displays the icon of the program in the far left, as well as tools in the Quick Launch bar.

- **Window controls**—In the upper-right corner of the program window are three tools to change the state of the window. Minimize reduces the window to the taskbar; Restore Down reduces the window to its previous smaller size (or, if the window is already at a smaller size, it changes to Maximize, which makes the window full size); and Close, which closes the file and, if no other files are open for that program, closes the program as well.

- **Ribbon**—The ribbon is a feature common to some legacy programs, offering the tools and options you need for working with various programs. You instead might see a menu bar listing menu names close to the top of the window. You can click a menu name to display a list of tools you can use in your program.

- **Scrollbars**—Depending on the size of your file and the type of program you are using, you might see horizontal and vertical scrollbars.

- **Work area**—The work area of the window is the place where you write documents, create worksheets, edit photos, and more. The file you open and work with appears in the work area.

Exploring a Windows 10 Universal App

Windows 10 universal apps have a new and improved look that makes the tools easy to find and the screen easy to navigate. The title bar and window tools (Minimize, Restore, and Close) are at the top of the screen. Along the left edge of the screen is the Expand button that "rolls out" the names of tools shown horizontally down the left side of the display.

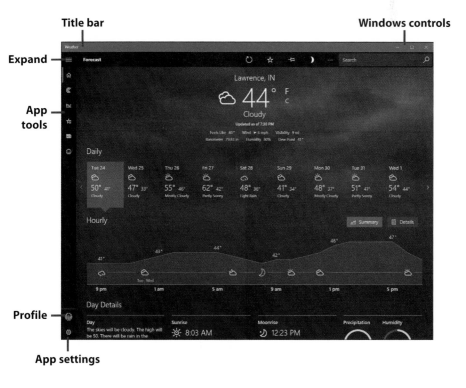

Working with an App

Virtually all universal apps have some consistent features you can work with by following these steps, which use the Weather app as an example.

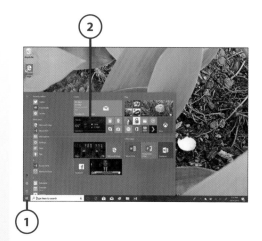

1. Click the Start button to open the menu.

2. Click the Weather app. The app opens fully on your screen.

3. Click the menu button in the upper left. The menu opens, showing you the names of the various tools in the toolbar on the left.

4. Click Settings. The settings for the Weather app appear.

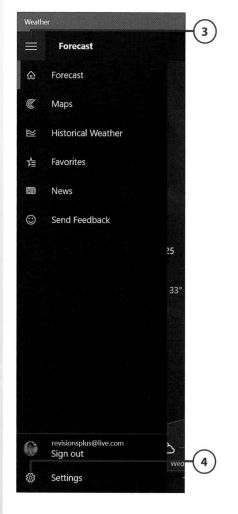

5. Click the arrow to return to the
main Weather app window.

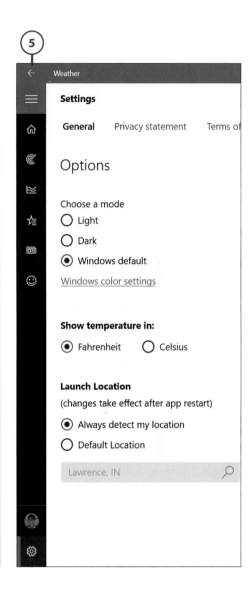

Snapping Apps

Snapping apps enables you to arrange two or more apps open on the screen
at once.

You can snap up to four apps depending on your screen's resolution, arranging them by dragging them with your finger, using the mouse, or using the
keyboard (the Windows key and the arrow keys) to position the apps where
you want them to appear.

Key Combinations for 2×2 Display

To place the app	Use these keystrokes
Upper-left corner	Win + left arrow, Win + up arrow
Upper-right corner	Win + right arrow, Win + up arrow
Lower-left corner	Win + left arrow, Win + down arrow
Lower-right corner	Win + right arrow, Win + down arrow

To make use of this feature, open the apps you want to use and drag each one to the corner in which you want it placed. Windows 10 positions each app in that quadrant of the screen so that you can work with them side by side.

Although Microsoft calls this feature 2×2—meaning two apps horizontal and two apps vertical—you don't have to have four apps open to use it. You can grab and "snap" an app into place on one side of the screen and do the same with another so you have two apps tiled on the screen. Or you can do the same with three apps—two on one side and one on the other. The feature is designed to be flexible, so experiment and see what's most comfortable for you.

Get Me Back to Full Screen

When you want to do away with the tiling effect, click the divider and drag it to the right, off the right edge of the screen. The app that was in the left window then becomes the only app visible on your screen. You can also make an app full screen quickly by double-clicking the title bar or clicking the Restore tool on the current app to enlarge it to Full Screen view.

It's Not All Good

FINDING THE SNAP FOR YOU

Depending on the device or computer you are using, not all snap features may work for you. For example, Windows 10 includes the Snap Assist, vertical snap, and 2×2 snapping, but only 2×2 snap works on my 2-in-1 tablet.

Snap Assist displays thumbnails of other open apps whenever you snap an app to the side of the screen, and vertical snap enables you to use the Windows key with up-, down-, right- or left-arrow keys to position the open app where you want it to appear on the screen.

Closing Apps

One of the jarring things about the earliest versions of Windows 8 was that you didn't need to close any app you had opened; there was no Close tool, and apps not in the current focus were said to go into suspension so they weren't using any active memory. That idea was just too bizarre for many Windows users.

So now, in Windows 10, the Close box is part of every app you work with, no matter what.

Closing Selected Apps

When you're ready to put away an app you've been working with, closing it is a simple matter. Follow these steps:

1. Select the app you want to close if you have more than one app displayed on the screen.

2. Click or tap the app's Close box.

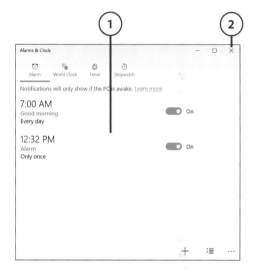

Save Before You Close

Many apps save their data as you work, but for those that don't, make sure to save any work you have in progress before you close the app.

Using the Task Manager

You can also close open apps using the Task Manager.

1. Press Ctrl+Alt+Delete and click Task Manager to display the Task Manager window. (You can also right-click the taskbar and select Task Manager from the shortcut menu that appears.)

2. Select the app you want to close.

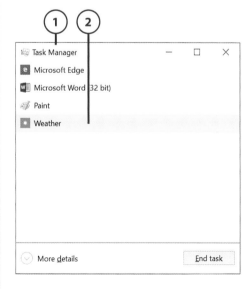

3. Select End Task to close the selected app.

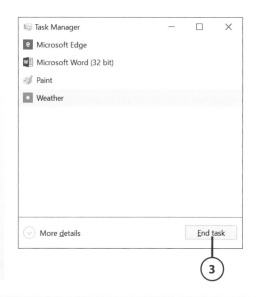

3

>>>Go Further

ADVANCED MANAGEMENT

The Task Manager can give you all kinds of information about how much processing power each app uses, but the super technical information is hidden by default in Windows 10. When you open Task Manager, you simply see which apps are running. You can then decide whether you want to see more information by clicking the More Details link at the bottom of the menu. These details can include showing how much processing power each open app is using and how that might be affecting the overall performance of your computer or device.

One great feature the detailed version of Task Manager offers is an evaluation of how much impact the apps you load automatically at startup are having on your computer's performance.

After you've enabled More Details, click the Startup tab at the top of the Task Manager dialog box. In the Startup Impact column, on the far right of the dialog box, you see how Windows 10 rates the impact the various apps have on the startup routine. If you see an app that is rated as having a High impact, you can select it and then tap or click Disable to keep it from loading automatically. You might find that Windows 10 boots faster after you've disabled high-impact apps. However, you should keep in mind that disabling these apps can prevent specific features and functions of your system from operating as intended.

Getting Apps from the Microsoft Store

The Microsoft Store is the place where you'll find all kinds of apps, games, media, and more to extend your digital experience whether you're using a computer, tablet, or phone. The Store includes lots of free apps as well as apps and media you can purchase. You can buy and watch seasons of your favorite TV shows, find and stream new music, even purchase and read ebooks—right in Windows 10.

You display the Microsoft Store by clicking the Store app on your Start menu or on the taskbar. When the Store opens, you see a number of suggested and popular apps (just in case you're in a shopping mood). You can also search for specific apps in the Store, browse through apps in different collections, take a look at the top-rated apps, get information about the apps you've already purchased and downloaded, and more.

Choose your media   **Tap to learn more**   **Search for an app**

Look through collections   **Scroll down to browse**

As you scroll down the Store page, you'll see that it displays a number of categories, including Today's Deals, Picks for You, Most Popular, Top Free Apps, Top Free Games, New Movies, Top-Selling TV Shows, New Books, and Collections. At the far right of each category is a Show All link. Click the link, and the Store displays all available apps or games in that category.

Searching for an App

To search for an app within the Microsoft Store, open the Store app and use the Search tool that appears in the upper-right corner.

1. Display the Microsoft Store.

2. Click in the Search box and type a word or phrase you want to search for. The Microsoft Store displays a short list of direct matches.

3. To see a broader range of results, click the magnifying glass. A results page appears, showing you all the apps and games that match your search phrase.

4. Refine the search by clicking the drop-down boxes and choosing options that further narrow the search results.

5. Review information about the app, including the price and the average user rating.

6. Click a tile to display more detailed information about the specific app.

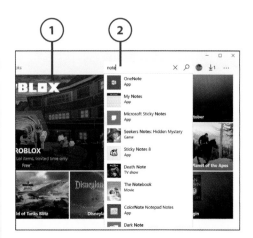

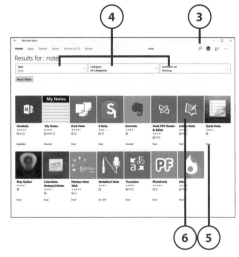

Reviewing and Installing an App

You can easily install an app you've found by tapping or clicking it, reading the description (and perhaps the user reviews, too), and then clicking the Install button. Don't forget to check the price, which appears just below the Install button in the top-left corner of the screen.

1. Find the app you want to view in the Microsoft Store and click the app tile. The app page opens.

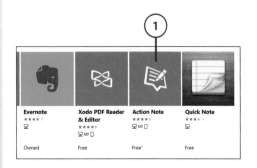

2. Scroll through the app information and decide whether you want to install the app.

3. Click Get to start the installation. Windows 10 shows you the status of the installation.

4. Click Pause to suspend the download.

5. Click the X to cancel the installation.

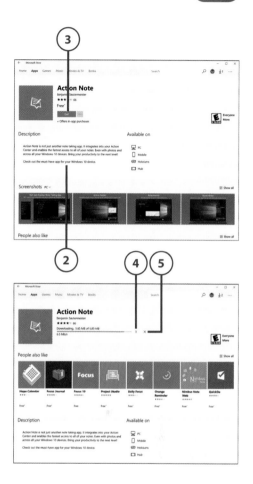

Opening an Installed App

When the installation is complete, the Get button changes to Launch, and you can click the button to launch the app on your Windows 10 PC or device. You might also see a Cortana notification that the app has been installed and is ready to launch.

Managing Your Apps

You can use the Microsoft Store app to see which apps you've purchased and installed, and you can easily update, install, or remove them as needed.

1. Display the Microsoft Store by clicking the Store app in the Windows 10 taskbar.

2. Click the See More button. A list of options appears.

3. Click Settings to change the way the Store displays information.

4. Click Purchased to see a list of all the apps you've purchased from the Microsoft Store.

5. Click My Library to see all the apps you've purchased and installed across all your Windows devices.

6. Click Downloads and Updates to see which apps you have that are ready for downloading and installing.

Updates Available

Apps might show up in your Downloads list when you have a version of an app for which an update is available. Click the Download button to the right of the app to update the app, or click the Trash icon to delete the update. If you want to check for updates for all your apps, click the Check for Updates button in the upper-right area of the screen.

Overseeing Your Finances in the Microsoft Store

The Microsoft Store also makes it easy for you to keep an eye on how much you're spending. You can access your account within the Microsoft Store and make any changes you need to on the fly.

1. Open the Microsoft Store and click Account at the top of the screen.

2. Click Purchased. The Order History page of your Microsoft account appears.

3. Review the recent transactions connected to your Microsoft account.

4. Click the Close box when you're finished reviewing your transactions.

Uninstalling Apps

To free up space on your hard drive and allow room for other programs, you can easily remove apps you no longer need.

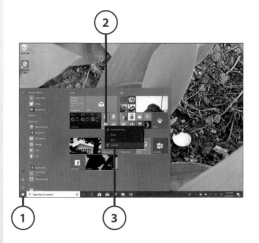

1. Display the Start menu and locate the app you want to uninstall.

2. Right-click the app or app tile to display the options menu.

3. Click Uninstall. Windows 10 displays a message box asking you to confirm the removal of the app.

4. Click Uninstall, and Windows 10 removes the app.

This app and its related info will be uninstalled.

Uninstall

You can pin favorite
folders to Quick Access.

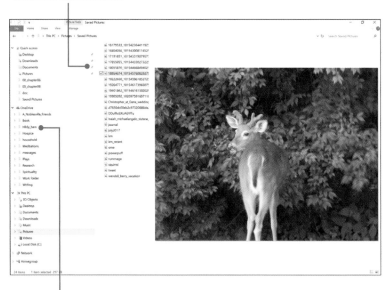

OneDrive folders appear
showing your files in the cloud.

This chapter shows you how to use File Explorer to organize your folders and files by exploring these tasks:

→ Getting started with File Explorer
→ Using the ribbon
→ Managing your files and folders
→ Copying, moving, and sharing files and folders
→ Using Files On-Demand with OneDrive

Working with Your Files in File Explorer and OneDrive

When you need to manage, copy, and organize files and folders in Windows 10, you use File Explorer to accomplish that task. This tool has been around as long as Windows has existed, although its name changed from Windows Explorer to File Explorer with the advent of Windows 8.

In Windows 10 Fall Creators Update, OneDrive—which is integrated with File Explorer so you can get to your cloud files easily—has gotten a development boost. Now OneDrive files are available to you "on-demand," which means you're able to see all your files when you view them in File Explorer, but OneDrive downloads and opens the files you need as you open them. This preserves disk space for you and makes it seamlessly easy for you to work with files anytime, anywhere.

This chapter introduces you to File Explorer and shows you how to save files to—and retrieve files from—your OneDrive folders in the cloud.

Getting Started with File Explorer

Sure, media and gaming are both big draws for computer and device users these days. But once upon a time most of us used our computers to get work done—to create, edit, and share files; to create and manage projects; to track sales and produce reports; and more.

Whether social media and movies have taken over a large percentage of your computer time or not, files and folders are still at the heart of computing for many people.

Working with the files you create is likely a daily reality, whether you are updating and sharing worksheets and documents or you need a way to manage your favorite media. File Explorer is the tool in Windows 10 you use to work with your many files and folders. Luckily, it's always within reach: You launch File Explorer from the taskbar or from the Start menu, which means you can get to it easily no matter what else you might be doing.

Starting File Explorer

The easiest way to launch File Explorer is to click or tap the File Explorer icon on the left side of the taskbar. File Explorer opens in a window on your screen.

**Click or tap to launch
File Explorer.**

Touring the File Explorer Screen

File Explorer is simple to use, and the tools are fairly intuitive. Across the top you see four tabs—File, Home, Share, and View—that contain the tools you'll use to work with your files and folders. The column on the far left is a Navigation pane that lists the different places your files are stored.

The Quick Access area is the place where you can pin all the folders you use most often—this way you can find them quickly anytime you need them.

The center column shows you the contents of the selected location, and the column on the right shows you more about a file selected in the center column.

Here are some of the key tools you'll be using in File Explorer:

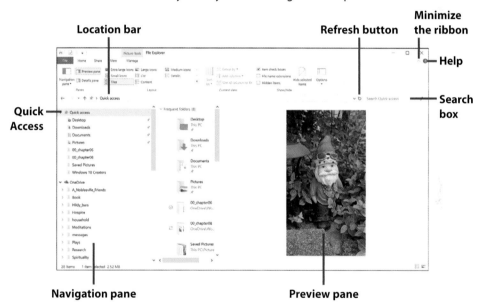

- **Location bar**—The Location bar shows the currently displayed folder.

- **Refresh button**—The Refresh button updates the list of files in the current folder.

- **Search box**—You can use the Search box to find folders and files in File Explorer.

- **Navigation pane**—The Navigation pane displays your favorites, folders, and files on your computer.

- **Quick Access**—Quick Access displays key folders and accounts, such as Office 365, that you use often. You can pin folders in the Quick Access area so you can reach them easily.

- **Preview pane**—The Preview pane shows an image of the file selected in the center column of File Explorer.

- **Minimize the ribbon**—Use this tool to both hide and display the File Explorer ribbon.

- **Get Help**—Click Get Help to display a pop-up window of help information related to the task you were performing in File Explorer.

Switching Between the Preview and Details Pane

You'll use the panel on the right side of File Explorer to get more information about a file you're working with. File Explorer changes what appears in that panel, depending on which view you have selected: the Preview pane or the Details pane. These two tools act as a toggle. When you click or tap the View tab and display the Preview pane, you see a preview of the contents of the file. When you tap or click the Details pane, the Preview pane is replaced by a pane that shows you when the file was last modified, what file size it is, whether the file is shared, and other file details.

Working with Quick Access

The Quick Access area in File Explorer gives you access to key folders and accounts connected to your computer or device. For example, you can get to your desktop, your Downloads folder, your Office 365 account, the Recycle Bin, and other folders you pin in place in the Quick Access area.

If your phone is connected to your Microsoft Account (and connected by USB to your PC), you're able to access the files on your phone by using File Explorer as well.

1. Click Quick Access in the Navigation pane.

2. Click the arrow to the left of Quick
   Access to display the items in the
   list.

3. Click any folder you want to view.

4. To pin a folder to Quick Access,
   right-click the folder you want to
   add.

5. Click Pin to Quick Access.

Unpinning Is a Snap

You can easily remove a folder
you no longer want pinned to
Quick Access by right-clicking the
folder and choosing Unpin from
Quick Access. You can also click
the Pin icon to the right of the
folder to unpin it.

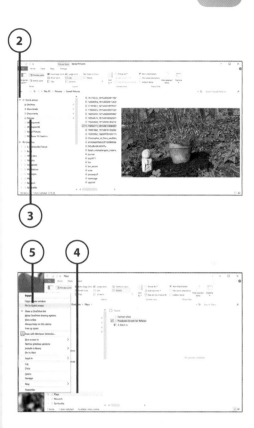

Checking Out This PC

This PC, located in the Navigation
pane, also gives you top-level access
to your content, organized by type or
location. The content is arranged by
category (what in earlier versions of
Windows we called libraries): Music,
Pictures, Documents, Videos, and
Downloads. This PC also shows you
at a glance which devices and drives
are connected to your PC.

1. Click or tap the arrow to the
   right of This PC in the Navigation
   pane. The list of primary folders
   appears.

2. Select the folder with the files you
   want to view.

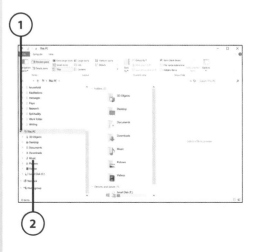

3. Click the arrow to display subfolders.

4. Click a file in the folder to see its Preview pane.

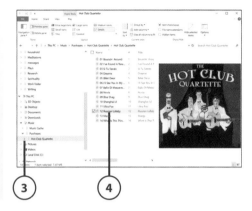

Changing the File Explorer Layout

You can hide and redisplay the various panes in File Explorer: Details, Preview, and Navigation. Tap or click the View tab and in the Panes group on the left of the ribbon, select the pane you want to display. If you deselect both the Preview pane and the Details pane, the center pane extends to show only the files and subfolders in the currently selected folder. You can also tap or click the Navigation pane arrow to display a menu of options for changing the way the Navigation pane displays folders and favorites. To redisplay a pane you've hidden, tap or click the name of the pane to select the one you want to show.

Using the Ribbon

The File Explorer ribbon offers the tools you need based on what you're trying to do. Even the major tabs change, depending on what you've selected. If you choose This PC, for example, the tabs that appear are File, Computer, and View. But if you select one of the folders in the This PC group, the tabs are File, Home, Share, and View.

In addition to the primary tabs, the File Explorer tab displays contextual tabs that appear only when you've selected a specific something. For example, when you click one or more picture files, the Picture Tools contextual tab appears above the ribbon. When you click outside the picture file, the Picture Tools tab disappears.

Learning the Ribbon Layout

The tabs in File Explorer group all the tools you need for working with your files and folders.

The File tab gives you access to the folders you use frequently. You can also work with the command prompt, delete the file history, display help, and close File Explorer.

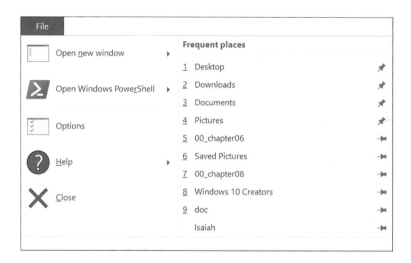

The Home tab provides common tools you'll use for copying and pasting files and paths; moving, deleting, and renaming files and folders; adding folders; opening files and folders; displaying file and folder properties; and selecting files and folders.

The Share tab contains tools for sharing the content you've selected, whether you want to email the files or folders, compress them into a zip file, share them with your HomeGroup, or fine-tune the security settings assigned to the file or folder.

The View tab includes tools you can use to change the way the File Explorer window appears. You can use the tools in the View tab to set up File Explorer the way you want it, displaying the Navigation pane, the Preview or Details panes, the size of the icons you want to use, and the data that will be either hidden or displayed. You can also add columns, sort files, and select from different layouts in the File Explorer screen.

Recognizing Contextual Tabs

You know when you're looking at a contextual tab on the File Explorer ribbon because it looks different from the regular tabs. The regular tabs are white and gray—the selected tab appears white, and the other tabs appear gray. When you've selected a file, a folder, or another object in File Explorer, a contextual tab related to the item you selected appears in another color along the top of the ribbon. When you click the contextual tab, you find tools that enable you to work specifically with the file or folder you've selected.

Showing and Hiding the File Explorer Ribbon

The ribbon contains the tools you use to work with your files and folders in File Explorer. Each tab contains a unique set of tools, and categories within the tabs group like tools. For example, in the Organize group of the Home tab are tools for moving and copying files to other folders. Additionally, the Organize group includes files for deleting and renaming files.

Some users prefer hiding the ribbon when they aren't working with it; this gives them a little more room to work with their files. The tool for hiding and displaying the ribbon is near the Help tool in the right side of the File Explorer window.

1. You can hide the ribbon by tapping or clicking the Minimize the Ribbon tool.

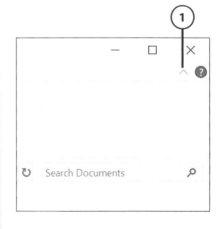

2. Display the ribbon by tapping or clicking the same tool, which is now called the Expand the Ribbon tool.

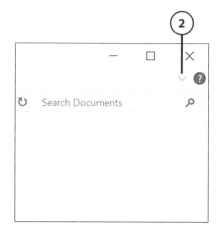

>>>Go Further
MORE TOOLS WITHIN REACH: THE QUICK ACCESS TOOLBAR

File Explorer also has a Quick Access toolbar in the upper-left corner of the Explorer window. The Quick Access toolbar gives you a small, customizable set of tools you can get to easily. It's always within easy clicking or tapping reach.

By default, the Quick Access toolbar in File Explorer shows only the Properties and New Folder tools, but you can tap or click the Customize Quick Access Toolbar arrow next to the New Folder tool to display options that enable you to add undo, redo, delete, and rename tools. To add a tool, click or tap the one you want to add to the toolbar. To remove a tool, tap or click the arrow again, and then tap or click a selected tool to remove the check mark. The tool is removed from the toolbar.

You also can choose a different position for the Quick Access toolbar by tapping or clicking the Customize arrow and selecting Show Below the Ribbon. This moves the Quick Access toolbar so that it appears beneath the ribbon but above the Location bar. There's also a command that suppresses the display of the ribbon in the Quick Access toolbar menu; to hide the ribbon, click or tap Minimize the Ribbon.

Get the Scoop on Your Tools

File Explorer also has hotkey ToolTips that tell you the name of the tool, give you a short description, and (in some cases) display the shortcut key for using the tool. All you need to do is hover the mouse over an item you're wondering about.

>>>Go Further
LIBRARY CHANGES IN WINDOWS 10

In previous versions of Windows, libraries in the Navigation pane offered you indexed locations of a specific type of files. The library gathered like files together so you could find them easily. When you clicked a library to view its contents, what you were really seeing were links to the files stored in their respective folders.

Libraries were phased out in Windows 8.1 because the primary folders in This PC enabled you to do basically the same tasks you performed with libraries. But if you like the convenience libraries offered, you can add them to the Navigation pane in Windows 10.

Click the Navigation Pane tool in the View tab and select Show Libraries. You can also create new libraries of your own by right-clicking or tapping and holding the folder you want to use to create a new library; then select Include in Library and select Create New Library.

Managing Your Files and Folders

Everything you need to do with files—copy them, rename them, put them in folders, and delete them—you can do in File Explorer. You can work with those files whether they are document files, picture files, media files—any type of file! You can easily create and move folders and store files both on your computer or device or in Web access.

Finding Files and Folders

File Explorer includes a comprehensive search tool that makes finding files and folders easy. You can enter a word or phrase in the Search box for a simple search or refine your search by searching for a specific date, kind of file, size, or other file properties.

1. Begin by tapping or clicking the folder (for example, Documents, Music, Pictures, or Videos) or the drive where you want to search.

2. Tap or click in the Search box, and type a word or phrase to describe what you're searching for. The Search Tools Search contextual tab appears above the ribbon.

3. In the Location group, tap or click whether you want to search your entire computer, the current folder, or all subfolders.

4. In the Refine group of the Search Tools Search tab, tap or click a search filter if you want to apply one: Date Modified, Kind, Size, or Other Properties.

5. Tap or click the search result you want to see.

6. If you want to repeat the search in a different location, select Search Again in the Location group and click or tap your choice.

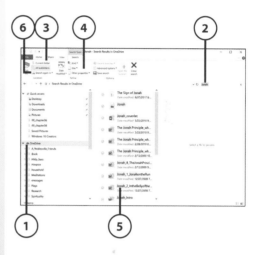

Finding Specific File Types

When you want to find files in a specific format—for example, .jpg, .wmv, .docx, or .mp3—use the Type filter in the Other Properties tool in the Refine group. When you click Type, File Explorer displays the word in the Search box. You can type the extension of the file type you want to find (.jpg, .png, etc.), and files with that type are displayed.

>>>*Go Further*

SAVING YOUR SEARCHES

If you find that you often perform the same searches—perhaps you search for the latest podcasts or look for the newest video clips that have been added to your computer—you can save the search so you can use it again later.

Enter the search information as usual, and then, when the search results appear in the File Explorer window, tap or click Save Search in the Options group of the Search Tools Search tab. The Save As dialog box appears. Type a filename for the saved search, and tap or click Save.

Now you can use the search at any time by tapping or clicking the saved search in the Quick Access area at the top of the Navigation pane.

Selecting Files and Folders

Selecting a file or folder might be as simple as clicking or tapping it. You might also need to select multiple files or folders to move to other places in File Explorer. The Home tab of File Explorer gives you the tools you need to select files and folders easily.

1. In the Navigation pane, click or tap the drive, Quick Access item, or folder where you want to select files.

2. Click or tap the Home tab.

3. If you want to select all contents of the selected folder, tap or click Select All in the Select group.

4. If you want to deselect any files or folders you've previously selected, click or tap Select None.

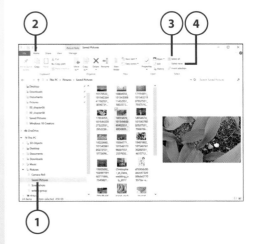

5. If you have previously selected multiple files (by pressing Ctrl and clicking files or tapping multiple selections) and want to change the selection to all those that were previously unselected, tap or click Invert Selection.

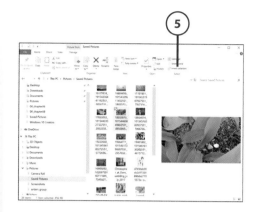

Viewing File Information

You can change the way you view the files in the folders you select by using the tools in the View tab.

The Panes group on the far-left side of the ribbon contains tools you can use to preview the selected file or display details about the file you've chosen.

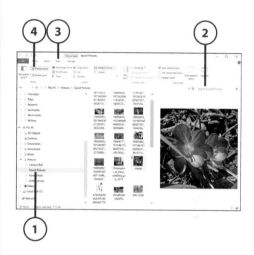

1. Click or tap the folder containing the file you want to see.

2. Use Search if necessary to locate the file.

3. Click or tap the View tab.

4. Tap or click Preview Pane in the Panes group if you want to see a preview of the file.

5. Tap or click Details Pane if you want to see the details of the file.

What Do You Mean, *Details?*

The Details pane of File Explorer gives you information about the selected file. You can see the filename, size, and date it was last modified. You can also see any tags that have been assigned to the file, review the authors' names, and (in some cases) see any rating that has been applied to the file.

Tagging Files

The information in the Details pane isn't just for viewing; you can also change the information and save it while you're there. By clicking or tapping in the Tags area and adding identifier tags, you can categorize your files so you can find them faster when you search for them later.

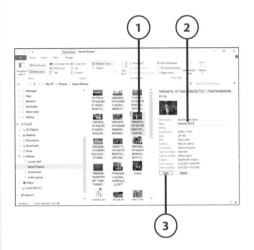

1. Select the file you want to tag in File Explorer.

2. In the Details pane, tap or click in the Tags field. Type tags you can use to identify or categorize the file, separating multiple tags with semi-colons.

3. Click or tap Save.

Tagging Again Later

The next time you add tags, when you tap or click in the Tag field and start typing, File Explorer displays a list box, suggesting tags you've entered previously. Click or tap the check box of any tag you want to add, and click or tap Save to save the tags.

>>>Go Further

RATING FILES

In the Details pane of your picture files, you can also assign a rating value to your image files. Rating the files on your computer helps you prioritize the ones you love over the ones you don't. This can help you select the right files when you're searching, for example, for the best photos you have of a particular event. If you've rated the files, you can search for the files with the highest rating, which gives you a results list that is the cream of the crop. Select the file you want to rate in File Explorer, and then click or tap the number of stars (one to five) you want to assign to the image. Tap or click Save to save your rating.

Arranging Folder Display

We all like to work in different ways. Some prefer working with thumbnails of our files; others want a simple list. Especially if you have many files in a folder, you might want to filter them so they appear in the order you prefer. You might also want to arrange them by the author or the date the file was last modified, for example.

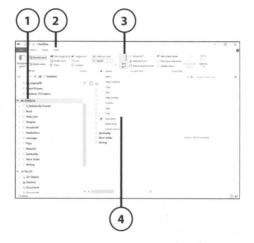

1. Click or tap the folder that contains the files you want to arrange in the Navigation pane.

2. Click or tap the View tab.

3. Click or tap the Sort By option in the Current View group. A list of options appears.

4. Click the setting that arranges the files the way you want them to appear. Authors lists the files and folders alphabetically by author; Date Modified lists files with the most recently modified files shown first; Tags arranges files alphabetically according to any tags you've assigned to the file; Type shows the files organized by file type; and Name lists the files alphabetically (from A to Z).

Any Folder Works

You may notice that the images for this example use OneDrive, which I cover at the end of this chapter. Files and folders in OneDrive work the same in File Explorer as any other file or folder on your computer.

>>>*Go Further*
DISPLAYING ADDITIONAL FOLDER DETAILS

You can display additional details about the files you're viewing in File Explorer—and use those columns to arrange the file list—by clicking the Add Columns tool in the Current View group of the View tab.

When you click Add Columns, you'll see a check mark to the left of the columns already included in the current view. For example, you might see checks in front of Date, Type, Size, Tags, and Authors. Other items, such as Date Created and Title, don't have checks. You can add them to your file display by clicking them. This enables you to show all files related to a particular topic, for example, or browse through files that were created after a particular date.

You can click Choose Columns in the Add Columns list to add specific column items to your display. The long list of choices you'll see includes items such as Country/Region, Cell Phone, Contributors, Lens Model, Status, and much more. In this way, you can customize the look and feel of your File Explorer view so it gives you all the information you need about your files in a way that matches the way you like to work.

Copying, Moving, and Sharing Files and Folders

Some of the practical tasks you'll need to perform regularly with File Explorer involve copying, moving, and sharing your files. Copying can be as simple as selecting a file, pressing Ctrl+C, and then pressing Ctrl+V to paste the file into the folder in which you want it to appear. File Explorer helps ensure you're not copying over existing files by prompting you if a copy conflict occurs.

Copying Files

You can use the Copy To tool in the Organize group of the Home tab to copy one or many files in the select-ed folder.

1. In the Navigation pane, click or tap the folder containing the files you want to copy.

2. Select the files or folders you want to copy.

3. Click or tap the Home tab.

4. Click or tap Copy To. A list of copy destinations appears.

5. Click the folder where you want to paste the files. File Explorer immediately copies the selected files to the location you selected.

6. If you want to create a new folder or scroll through a list of possible folders, select the file you want to copy, click Copy To, and select Choose Location. The Copy Items dialog box appears.

7. Click the arrow to display subfold-ers.

8. Click the folder where you want to copy the selected files.

9. Click Make New Folder if you want to copy the files to a new folder.

10. Click Copy to complete the opera-tion.

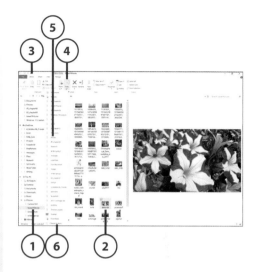

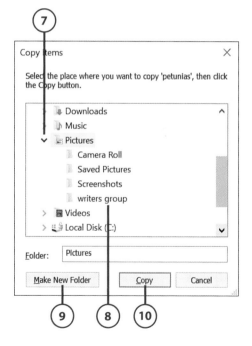

>>>Go Further
SOLVING COPY CONFLICTS

When you inadvertently try to copy two files with the same name into the same location, File Explorer prompts you to resolve the conflict. This can happen easily when you are moving files from one computer to another. Which file is the most recent one? File Explorer helps you make the call in the Replace or Skip Files dialog box. File Explorer gives you the option of going ahead with the copy and overwriting the existing file, skipping the copy procedure, or comparing the information for both files to see which one you want to keep.

Sharing Files

When you're ready to share your files with friends, family, and co-workers, select the file or group of files you want to share and tap or click the Share tab. You'll find tools that enable you to print, email, fax, burn to disc, or share the files with others in your HomeGroup (or who have accounts on your computer). Windows 10 includes a Share tool in the Send group of the Share tab.

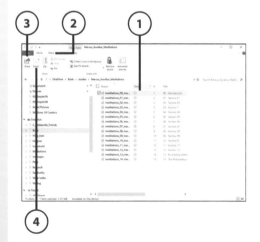

1. Select the file or files you want to share.

2. Click or tap the Share tab.

3. In the Send group, click Share. The panel on the right opens, offering the ways you can share the file. Depending on the type of file you've selected and the means of sharing available to you, you may be able to share only with your phone or another app.

4. Click Email if you want to share the file through email.

5. Click Zip if you want to compress the selected file(s).

6. If you want to stop sharing selected files, click Remove Access.

7. Fine-tune your security settings by clicking or tapping Advanced Security and adjusting the permission levels assigned to those you're sharing the files with.

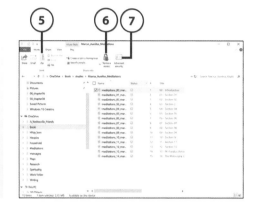

Sync Your File Explorer Settings

When you select the Sync Your Settings tool in the Account category of Windows 10 Settings, you can sync your File Explorer options and preferences along with the other Windows settings that are synced from computer to computer. This feature is available only if you log in to your computer using your Microsoft Account. Find out more about syncing your settings in Chapter 6, "Securing Your Computer—for Yourself and Your Family."

Moving Files: Looks Familiar

Moving files is very similar to copying files. You navigate to the folder containing the files you want to move, select them, and click Move To in the Organize group of the Home tab. You see the trusty folder list, where you can select the destination folder to which you want to move the files. Or you can click or tap Choose Location to display the Move Items dialog box, where you can choose a folder or subfolder—or add a new folder—you want to move the selected files to. Click Move to finish the job.

Compressing and Extracting Your Files

Sometimes when you want to email a bunch of files, it's easier to compress them into one file you can attach to an email message instead of attaching 10 or 12 different documents. After the recipient receives the compressed file, he needs to extract the contents. File Explorer includes tools to do both of those jobs: compressing and extracting files.

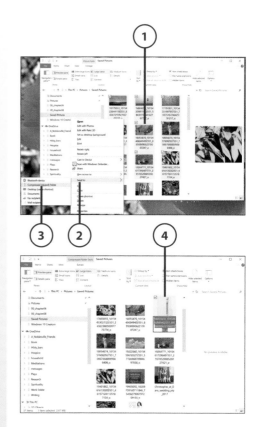

1. Select the files you want to include in the compressed file.

2. Right-click your selection and point to Send To.

3. Click Compressed (Zipped) Folder. File Explorer compresses the files and displays the zipped file with the name highlighted.

4. Type a new name for the compressed file.

5. To see and extract the contents of a compressed file, double-click or double-tap it.

6. Click or tap Extract All. The Extract Compressed (Zipped) Folders dialog box appears.

7. Click Browse if necessary to choose a folder for the extracted files. (It's okay to leave the default setting if that folder is where you want the uncompressed files to be placed.)

8. Click Extract. File Explorer extracts the files and places them in the folder you specified, ready to use.

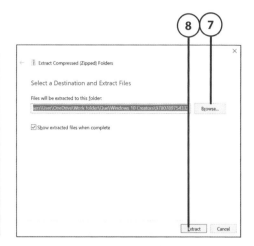

Using Files On-Demand with OneDrive

OneDrive is Microsoft's cloud storage service, and it works similarly to other such services, such as Apple's iCloud and Dropbox. Cloud storage allows you to automatically sync files and folders from your local hard drive to the Internet. Making use of this feature has two benefits. One, files stored in the cloud are available to you anywhere you have an Internet connection. Two, if something happens to the data stored locally on your computer, that data remains safe in the cloud.

The big news for OneDrive in Windows 10 Fall Creators Update is that now OneDrive accesses and displays your files "on-demand," meaning you can view the files and folders in File Explorer, but the files won't actually be downloaded to your computer or device unless you open them. So the files are retrieved on an as-needed basis, which saves disk space while not costing you any wait time.

OneDrive Support

You can access data stored on OneDrive from virtually any device or computer. iOS and Android have OneDrive apps and, when in doubt, you can access OneDrive data from any web browser by navigating to https://onedrive.live.com/.

To access OneDrive, you need to set up a Microsoft Account, as I discussed earlier in this book. When you log in to your computer using a Microsoft

Account, you have immediate access to your OneDrive data through File Explorer. OneDrive shows up in the navigation pane on the left, just below the Quick Access area.

Early in 2016, Microsoft changed the amount of storage available with One-Drive because some users were taking advantage of the "free, unlimited" storage space and posting entire movie collections and more. To gain some control over space management, Microsoft instituted the following changes:

- Free OneDrive storage is now set to 5 GB for all users.

- Previous paid storage plans for 100 GB and 200 GB are being discontin-ued, and the new rate is $1.99 per month for 50 GB.

- Office 365 Home, Personal, or University subscriptions include 1 TB of OneDrive storage as part of the monthly subscription fee.

Want to Know More?
You can find out more about the latest OneDrive changes by following the OneDrive Blog at http://blog.onedrive.com.

Local Accounts
If you use a Local account to log in to Windows, you can still access your OneDrive data through its website.

Because OneDrive is integrated into File Explorer, all the procedures you read earlier in this chapter work with your OneDrive folders. You can copy, paste, and edit files in your OneDrive just as with anyplace else on your computer.

Working with OneDrive in the Taskbar

In addition to seeing OneDrive listed in the Navigation panel in File Explorer, you can also access OneDrive—and check on things like file syncing and settings—by using the OneDrive icon on the right side of the taskbar, in the notifications area.

1. Click or tap the OneDrive icon. A pop-up list appears.

2. The list shows the files that are currently being uploaded to OneDrive.

3. Notice the status of the syncing process.

4. If you want OneDrive to display all your files and folders in the cloud (but only open the ones you select on-demand), click Show All Files.

5. Click the Settings button to open OneDrive settings.

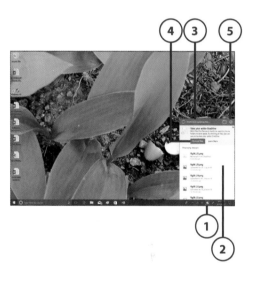

From Start to OneDrive

You can also launch OneDrive directly from the Start menu if you choose. Click or tap the Start button and choose the OneDrive tile or scroll down to OneDrive in the apps list and click the selection. File Explorer opens, and the OneDrive folder is selected. Now you can copy, move, or search your files normally.

Now Edge hides away open pages until you
need them, giving you more space on-screen.

You can now read ebooks
in Microsoft Edge and use
the Read Aloud tool to turn
them into audio books.

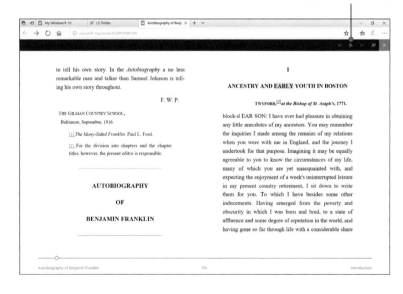

In this chapter, you learn how to use Microsoft Edge to get things done online. Specifically, you explore the following tasks:

→ What's new about Microsoft Edge
→ Getting to know today's Microsoft Edge
→ Browsing and searching the Web
→ Personalizing your browsing
→ Saving your favorites
→ Saving and working with Web content
→ Securing your browsing experience

Streamlined Surfing with Microsoft Edge

Microsoft Edge was introduced with an early update of Windows 10, and the browser has been gaining ground in the months since. Each version of Edge adds new features that show that Microsoft is taking user preferences seriously, understanding that we want our browsing experience to be safe, uncluttered, and just the way we like it.

Microsoft Edge in Windows 10 2017 Fall Creators Update includes several new features that extend what we can use the browser to do and make it more convenient to do it. A new tab process makes it easier to view and move among open pages (while still giving you maximum browsing room on-screen), and support for ebooks (PDFs and ePubs) make it a natural for you to read (or even listen to) your favorite ebooks whenever the mood strikes.

This chapter takes a close look at Microsoft Edge and shows you techniques for browsing, searching, saving, annotating, and working with content online.

What's New About Microsoft Edge?

Just a couple of iterations ago, Microsoft Edge was a completely new browser, approaching the new interconnected web-browsing world with a sleek design and minimal disruptions. The browser continues to grow and evolve, and developers have focused on ease of use and security for its users.

All browsers need to have certain capabilities—such as tools like search, the ability to add favorites or bookmarks, and customizable security features that enable users to feel safe while browsing. Microsoft Edge continues to build on its focus on safety and ease of use by improving the user experience online and working hard behind the scenes to make sure malware doesn't get through.

New features for Microsoft Edge in Windows 10 2017 Fall Creators Update include a clever new way of managing open tabs. Each web page you open appears in its own tab, and if you have a number of pages open at once, that can be pretty cumbersome and take up some on-screen space. Now developers have come up with a way to sweep away the tabs until you need them so they don't clutter up the space but are still easy to use and navigate.

With the growing success of electronic books, or ebooks, Microsoft Edge now makes it simple for you to read ebooks in their native formats—PDF or ePub—without any special app or ereader installed. To go along with this new feature in Edge, the Microsoft Store now has gone into the ebook business and has thousands of current and popular titles. There's also a "read aloud" feature in Microsoft Edge that enables you to listen to your ebook instead of reading it if you choose.

Getting to Know Today's Microsoft Edge

Whether you are using a mouse-driven system or navigating by touch, your basic browsing experience will feel familiar in Microsoft Edge. Some of the features you'll want to try include the following:

Read an ebook   **Choose a new page**   **Display the Hub**

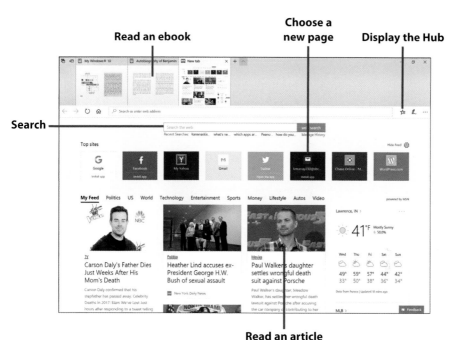

Search

Read an article

- Search in the address bar.

- Use the Hub to display your Favorites, Reading List, History, and Downloads, and find things you collect on the Web.

- Turn on Reading view to hide ads, links, and more so your article content is clear and easy to read.

- Write on web pages using Notes, and save your notes for later.

- Read or listen to an ebook in your browser window.

- Let Cortana help you with online searches for more information.

- Import your favorites and bookmarks from other browsers into Microsoft Edge.

- Choose a new dark theme for Microsoft Edge.

- Create your own start page.

- Let Microsoft Edge save your passwords and fill in forms for you.

Starting Microsoft Edge

Microsoft Edge is available on your Start menu. The Microsoft Edge icon is also available in the taskbar, which means you can easily launch the browser with a single click.

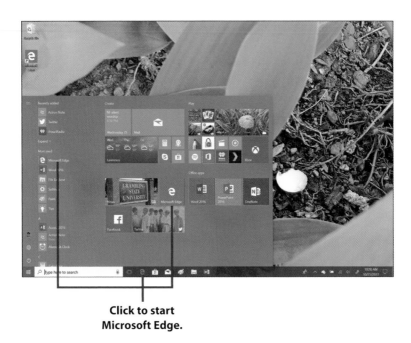

**Click to start
Microsoft Edge.**

Exploring Microsoft Edge

Microsoft Edge includes the basic browsing tools you would expect from a web browser, but this browser takes things a step further, giving you what you need to get things done quickly. Now you can use the address bar both for searches and for moving to a specific site; you can choose Reading view to suppress ads to make reading content easier; you can add Web Notes to pages; save Favorites and articles easily; and more.

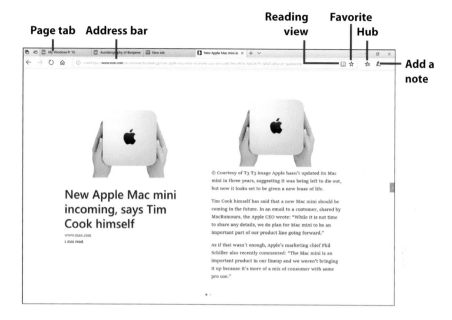

- **Address bar**—Click and search for information or browse the Web by tapping or clicking and typing in the same box.

- **Page tab**—Each web page is displayed in a separate tab, so you can have multiple pages open at once and move among them easily.

- **Reading view**—Click Reading view when you want to display web page content without ads, sidebars, and the like.

- **Favorite**—Click Favorites to save a web page or article to your Favorites or your Reading List.

- **Hub**—The Hub displays a pane that displays your Favorites, Reading List, History, Downloads, and Books.

- **Add Notes**—You can add notes to web pages using a pen or highlighter or click and add text notes to a page. You can then save the notes to access later or share with others.

No Place Like Home

You can add a Home button to your browser window if you'd like to be able to easily go back to your start page in Microsoft Edge. Click the Settings and More tool in the far-right side of the browser window, and then click Settings. Scroll down and click View Advanced Settings, and drag the Show the Home Button slider to the On position.

Browsing and Searching the Web

Chances are good that you're no stranger to browsing the Web. Whether you're shopping online, looking for a movie, updating social media, or chatting with friends, you probably are familiar with ways to get where you want to go and do what you want to do. This section provides some of the basic navigation techniques using the tools in Microsoft Edge.

Starting at the Top

The address bar at the top of the browser window is the place where all the action begins in your browser. Now you can also search for content, refresh the page, and go to specific web pages by entering information in the address bar.

1. Click in the Search or Enter Web Address box.

2. Begin typing the name of the site or the web address if you know it.

AutoComplete

Microsoft Edge attempts to autocomplete the phrase for you, so if you want to use the site provided, tap or click the suggestion that fits. If not, just keep typing the full address.

>>>Go Further

KEYBOARD SHORTCUTS FOR BROWSING

If you'd rather skip the clicking and navigate through the Web using your keyboard, you can use the following shortcut keys in Microsoft Edge:

- Press Ctrl+D to add another web page to your favorites.

- Press Ctrl+E to start a search in the address bar.

- Press Ctrl+F to search for content on the current web page.

- Press Ctrl+H to view your browsing history.

- Press Ctrl+L to highlight the search or address in the address bar.

- Press Ctrl+J to display the Download Manager.

- Press Ctrl+ the tab number to move to a different open tab.

Navigating the Web

Whether you're using Microsoft Edge or another browser, chances are good you already know how to move forward or backward from page to page. Here are the basic tools:

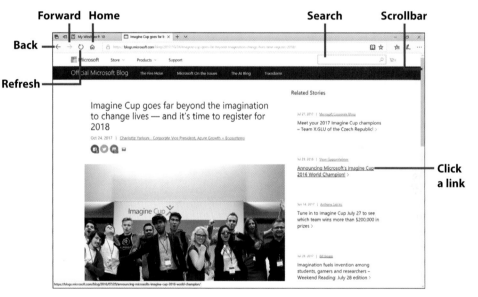

- **Back**—Tapping or clicking the Back button takes you back to the page you were previously viewing.

- **Forward**—Tapping or clicking Forward takes you to the web page you previously viewed after viewing the current one. This capability is helpful if you're moving back and forth between pages. If you haven't moved ahead to another page yet, this button is not available for you to click or tap.

- **Refresh**—Click the Refresh tool when pictures are downloading slowly or content on a web page doesn't look quite right. This reloads the page, which is likely to fix the problem.

- **Click a link**—Click or tap a link on the page to move to another page or perform a web action. What that link does—for example, whether it displays a new page, opens a document, or plays a media clip—depends on what the website designer programmed the link to do.

- **Search the site**—Many sites include a Search tool near the top of the site so that users can easily locate what they are looking for.

- **Scroll or swipe down the page**—Whether you are using a mouse or using touch, you can scroll or swipe down the page to display additional content.

Opening a New Tab

The process of opening a tab in Microsoft Edge is probably familiar. This enables you to view another web page in addition to the one—or ones—you're already viewing.

1. In the browser window, click or tap the New Tab icon to the right of the current tab.

2. In the New Tab page, you can see site panels of Top Sites across the page, as well as a Search box. Click the tile of the site you want to visit.

3. Type a word or phrase or enter the web address of the site you want to display. Alternatively, click the tile of the site you want to visit.

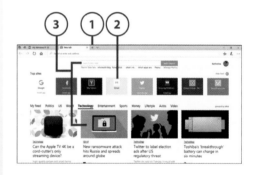

Tweaking the New Tab Display

You can change the New Tab window by clicking the Customize tool on the far right of the window and choosing content you'd like to see displayed whenever you click New Tab. On the Customize page, you can choose whether you want to see top sites, top sites and the news feed, or only a blank page when you click New Tab. For tabs that are already open, you can display a quick description of a tab's contents by hovering the mouse pointer over the tab.

Pinning Open a Tab

You can pin a tab to the browser window so that it always opens automatically whenever you launch Microsoft Edge. You might pin to your browser window your favorite news site, a stock tracker, or a weather site you visit regularly to help you be prepared for the day.

1. Open Microsoft Edge and display the web page you'd like to add to the browser.

2. Right-click the tab at the top of the browser window.

3. Click Pin.

Displaying and Hiding Tabs

Having tabs at the top of the web browser so you can move easily among open pages is a good idea. But once you get a number of pages open, it might be hard to remember the contents of each one. For this reason, developers have come up with a cool idea that allows you to peek at open pages without switching to them. You can display and hide tabs easily, or click to make a new page tab active without playing the hide-and-seek game.

1. Click the Show Tab Previews tool at the top of the browser window.

2. Review the open tabs and click the page you want to make active.

3. Click the Hide Tab Previews tool to hide the tabs.

>>>*Go Further*

QUIET SURFING WITH INPRIVATE BROWSING

In some cases, you might not want to track your browsing activity for others to see. Perhaps you're shopping for a holiday gift for someone and you don't want him to inadvertently discover it. You can turn on InPrivate Browsing to tell Microsoft Edge to skip recording your web activity. This means that the sites you visit won't be available in your browsing history, cookies, form data, temporary Internet files, or the usernames and passwords Microsoft Edge usually keeps.

Click the Settings and More tool and, in the menu that appears, click New InPrivate Window. Microsoft Edge opens a new browser session independent of the current one you have been using, and none of your browsing information is stored in the new session. When you're ready to end the InPrivate Browsing session, close the browser session.

Searching in Microsoft Edge

In Microsoft Edge, you can click in the Search or Enter Web Address box at the top of the screen and type a word or phrase that describes what you'd like to find.

1. Click or tap in the Search box and type a word or phrase describing what you want to find.

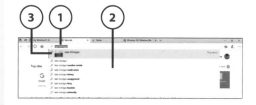

2. Your search provider, which is Bing until you change it (see the "Adding Search Providers" task later in this chapter), displays a list of search results, ranked from those that best match your search phrase to those that are not as close a match.

3. Click or tap a link you'd like to view.

Using Cortana in Searches

Cortana is also a part of Microsoft Edge, integrating your personal digital assistant with your every-day browsing experience. Cortana can help you make reservations, find a restaurant, or even search for content online. Before Cortana will work with Edge, however, you must have turned on the feature. Display Windows 10 Settings, choose Cortana, and make sure the Hey Cortana slider is in the On position.

1. Display a web page where you want to ask for Cortana's help.

2. Right-click the link you want to know more about.

3. Click Ask Cortana. Cortana displays a pane of information related to the item you selected.

4. You can review the information and click one of the links to find out more.

5. You can pin the panel open in your browser window by clicking the Pin This Pane tool.

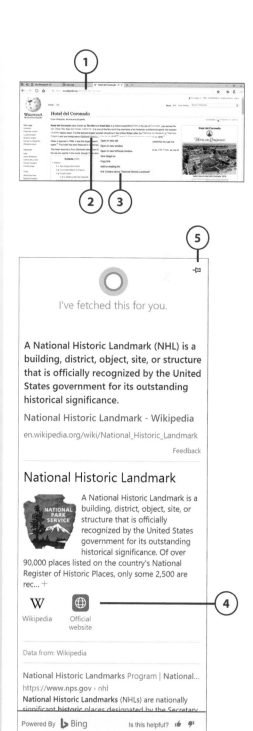

Adding Search Providers

If you prefer to use a different search engine instead of Bing with Microsoft Edge, you can easily add your favorite search provider and even make it the default if you'd like. Of course, Microsoft recommends that you stick with Bing because Windows 10 apps are linked directly to it with the idea of giving you useful, relevant, up-to-date information. But because Microsoft Edge uses OpenSearch technology, you can choose your own search provider at will. Here's how to do that:

1. In your web browser, display the search engine you want to add to Microsoft Edge.

2. Click the Settings and More tool in the browser window.

3. Click Settings.

4. Scroll down and click View Advanced Settings.

5. In the Search in the Address Bar With setting, click the Change Search Engine button.

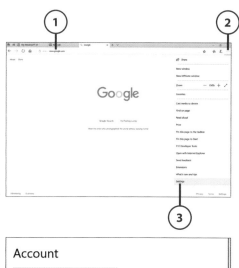

Account

Sync your favorites, reading list, top sites, and other settings across your Windows devices

On

Device sync settings

Advanced settings

View advanced settings

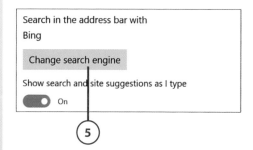

Search in the address bar with
Bing

Change search engine

Show search and site suggestions as I type

On

6. In the list, click the search provider that you want to use.

7. If you want to set the selected search provider as your default, click the Set as Default button.

8. To remove the search provider from the list, click Remove.

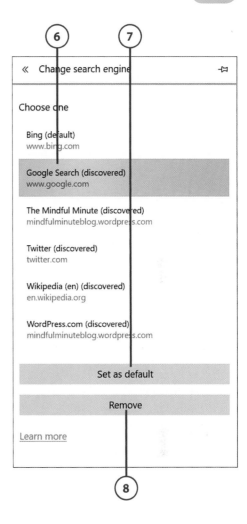

It's Not All Good

SEARCH ENGINES MISSING IN ACTION

You might notice that some of the big search engines you expected to see in this list are missing. This is because the Microsoft Edge engine supports only those search providers who use the OpenSearch standard. OpenSearch is a set of technologies published originally by Amazon.com that allows search results to be aggregated and shared in a standard and easy-to-understand format. You can find out more by going to www.opensearch.org.

Personalizing Your Browsing

Microsoft Edge includes a number of features you can use to tweak your browsing experience so that your browser looks and acts the way you want it to. You might want to change the theme from light to dark, zoom in or out on the content, or use the new Hub to display a pane of commonly used browsing tools and content. You can also set up your browser to start with the page or pages you're most interested in seeing.

Choosing a Theme

Microsoft Edge includes an alternative theme you can use to change the look of your browsing experience. By default, the browser window is displayed using the Light theme, but you can choose the Dark theme instead.

1. In the browser window, click the Settings and More tool.

2. Click Settings.

3. Click the Choose a Theme down arrow and click Dark. The browser window and the pane change to display the new theme.

Easier on the Eyes

Some people like to work with white text on a black background because they feel it is easier to read and causes less wear and tear on their eyes, especially at night. In Windows 10 Fall Creators Update, developers have included a new feature called Night Light that softens the screen lighting to take the need of your eyes into account when you're using your computer at night. You'll find the Night Light setting in the Display category of the Settings window.

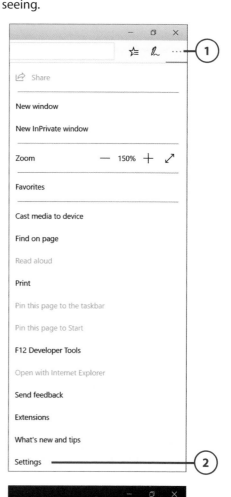

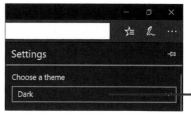

Magnifying and Reducing the View

Now you can easily magnify or reduce the size of the content on a web page by changing the view on-the-fly.

1. Click the Settings and More tool.

2. In the Zoom tool row, click Zoom Out to reduce the size of the content on the page.

3. Click Zoom In to magnify it. The page view changes by 25% each time you click one of the tools.

4. Click Full Screen to fill the computer or device screen with the web page. Browser tools will be visible. To remove the page from Full Screen view, press F11.

Selecting Your Start Page

If you have a particular web page you like to start your day with, you can make it your start page in Microsoft Edge. You'll find the tools you need in the Open With area of the Settings pane.

1. Click the Settings and More tool and choose Settings to display the Settings panel.

2. Click the Open Microsoft Edge With arrow and click A Specific Page or Pages.

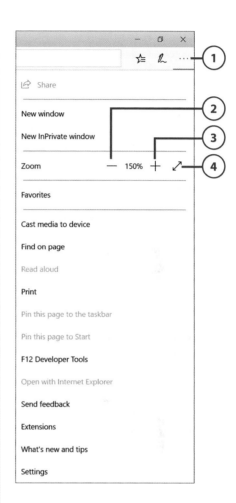

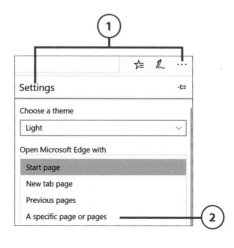

3. A web address box opens so you can enter the address for the new start page. (You can also choose one of the listed default options.) Type the web address for the page you want to use as your start page.

4. Click the Save tool to add the page.

Using the Hub

The Hub in Microsoft Edge enables you to move easily to content you've saved for later viewing.

1. Click the Hub tool on the taskbar of the browser window.

2. Click the tool that corresponds to the pane you want to see: Favorites, Reading List, Books, History, or Downloads.

3. Review the content in the list and click the article or page you want to view.

Erasing History

You can erase your past in Microsoft Edge by displaying the Hub, clicking the History tool, and choosing Clear History. In the Clear Browsing Data pane, enable or disable the check boxes next to the items you want to clear. Click or tap Clear. When Edge is done, you see the All Clear! message underneath the Clear button.

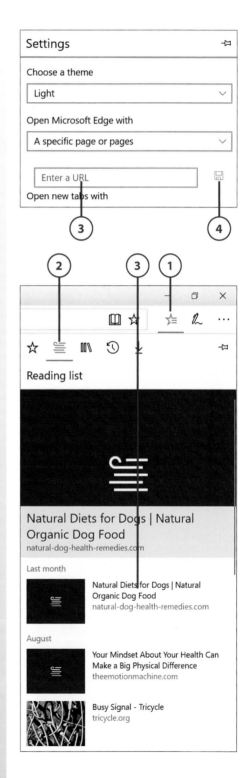

Working with Extensions

In the latest update of Windows 10, developers added support for extensions, which means the browser now works with add-on utilities designed to help you work with specific third-party sites and programs. For example, you can add an extension to optimize your Amazon.com shopping experience. Or you can install the Office Online extension, so you can work with your Office files within your browser without ever needing to open an Office application.

Adding an Extension

The Settings and More pane in Microsoft Edge includes a new option that takes you directly into the world of extensions.

1. Click Settings and More on the right side of the browser window.

2. Click Extensions.

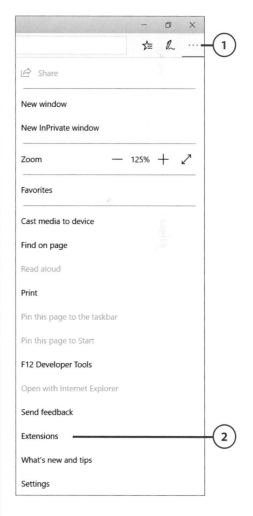

3. Click Get Extensions from the Store.

4. Scroll through the list of available extensions, and click or tap one you like. A page opens explaining more about the extension.

5. To download the extension, click the Get button. The extension is downloaded to your browser. After the download is complete, the Launch button appears, and you can click or tap it to start the extension.

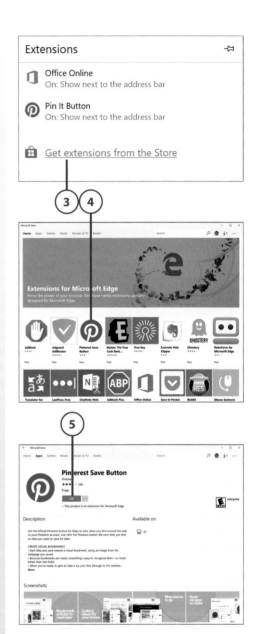

Turning On Extensions

Once you have downloaded and installed the extensions you want to use with Microsoft Edge, you need to tell the browser you're ready to use them. Note that you can disable extensions at any time you like by returning to the Extensions panel in the Settings and More pane in Microsoft Edge.

1. In the Extensions page of the Settings and More pane, Microsoft lets you know you have a new extension.

2. Click Turn It On to activate the extension.

Using Extensions

Depending on which extension you've installed, the way in which you use it varies. The extension tool appears to the right of the address bar in the browser window, and what happens when you click or tap the tool depends on what the extension is programmed to do.

For example, Office Online, opens a list that gives you access to your most recent Office documents. To use the Pinterest Pin It extension, you click the Pin It button.

1. Click the extension you want to use.

2. Click the file you want to open or the action you want to take.

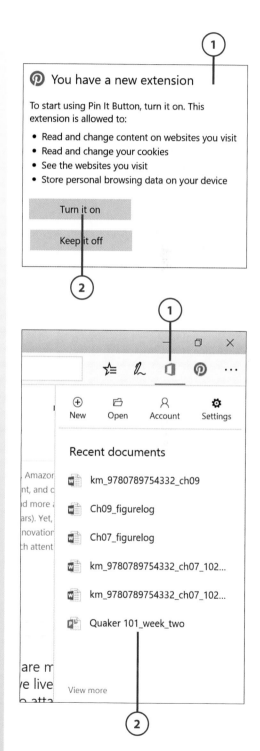

Saving Your Favorites

We all have favorite websites we visit frequently. You might like to start your day with a favorite news or social media site. There's likely one website you use when you need to look up a recipe and another you go to for the latest sports news. Perhaps you do a lot of shopping on a favorite discount site. You can save all these sites you use often as favorites so you can find them easily whenever you need them.

Adding a Favorite

You can easily add a favorite site to your Favorites list in Microsoft Edge. When you add the site to your list, you can also change the name of the site if you like.

1. Navigate to the web page you want to add as a favorite.

2. Click the Favorites tool in the browser toolbar.

3. Click in the Name box, and type a name for the favorite if you don't want to use the default.

4. Click in the Save In box, and choose a folder for the favorite.

5. Click Add to save the favorite.

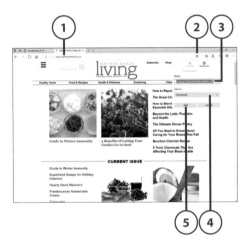

Creating Folders

If you save a lot of favorite sites, folders can help you keep them all organized, but you don't have to use them.

Saving and Backing Up Your Favorites

If you have logged in to your computer or device using your Microsoft account, Microsoft Edge saves and backs up your browser favorites automatically so you can access them no matter which computer or device you may be using. Nice!

Importing Favorites from Other Browsers

In Microsoft Edge you can import favorites you've saved in other browsers as well, and those favorites are available across all your Windows 10 computers and devices for which you've logged in using a Microsoft account.

1. Display Settings by clicking the Settings and More tool, scrolling down, and choosing Settings.

2. Click the Import from Another Browser button.

3. Click the Import button. If prompted, choose the browser from which you want to import the favorites. Microsoft Edge displays an All Done! message when the process is complete, and the imported favorites should now be available in your Favorites list.

Quick Imports

You can also import favorites by displaying the Hub and clicking the Favorites tool. Click Settings to display the Settings pane where you can import content from other browsers into Microsoft Edge.

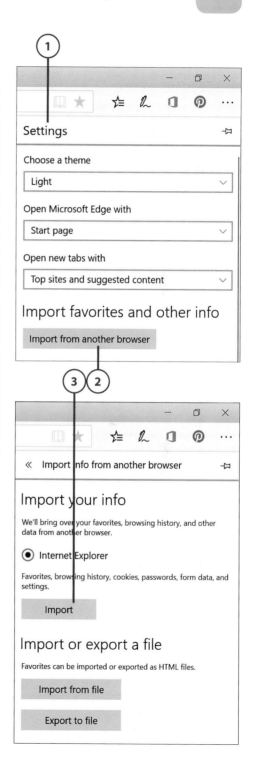

Saving and Working with Web Content

Microsoft Edge includes some exciting new features to make your web browsing experience easier and more productive. The new Reading view enables you to clear away ads so that you can focus on the real content on the page. Reading List tracks and syncs articles you want to read online so you can return to them when you're ready—on any of your Windows 10 devices.

The Notes tool enables you to make notes and drawings on web pages and then save them and share them with others. A whole new makeover in the printing department enables you to tweak your page printouts so you get the web content you want in a readable format.

Reading Clearly in Reading View

Most of us know that feeling of frustration that comes when we're looking for something specific online and we have to read around so many ads on the page it's hard to find what we need. Reading view helps clear away the clutter.

1. Display the page you want to read.

2. Click the Reading view tool in the right side of the browser window. The page changes to put the content front and center, with no ads or side columns.

Changing to Reading View on-the-Fly

If you don't want to reach for the mouse and click to display Reading view, press the key combination Ctrl+Shift+R to turn on Reading view. To turn Reading view off, press the key combination again.

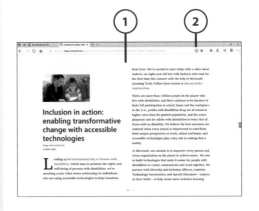

Adding eBooks

The Reading View feature makes reading content online an easier and more pleasant task (without all the distractions of advertisements). To build on that improvement, Edge now supports ebooks in their native formats: PDF and ePub. You don't need any special ereader or app to read your favorite books. And the Microsoft Store now includes thousands of titles (some free) that you can download and read whenever you choose.

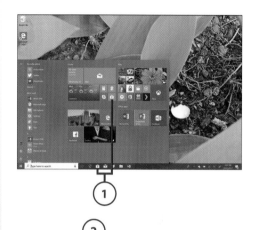

1. Launch the Microsoft Store by clicking the Store icon in the taskbar or on the Start screen.

2. In the Microsoft Store, click Books.

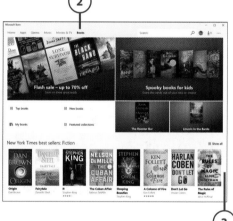

3. Scroll through the book listings and find a book you want to read. Toward the bottom of the Books page, you see a tile for Free Classics; click that to be taken to a page of free classic titles. Click the book you want to read and click Get to add the book to your library.

   You may be prompted for your Windows login password. Otherwise, click Get to choose the book. Even though the title is free, you still have to agree to the Store Terms of Agreement.

4. Click Read to download the title to the Books pane in the Edge window.

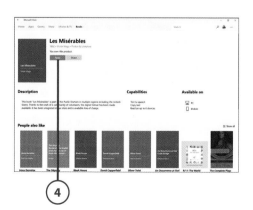

Reading eBooks in Your Browser Window

Once you've chosen and added the book you want to read to your library in Microsoft Edge, you can find the title in the Books tab of the Hub. Edge stores settings related to your book reading experience, so you can read as long as you like, and when you're done, Edge marks your place so you can continue on from that point later.

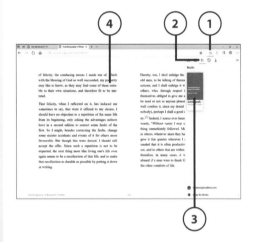

1. In the Microsoft Edge window, click the Hub tool.

2. Click or tap Books. Your ebook appears in the panel.

3. Click or tap the book to open it in your browser window.

4. Read the book in the browser.

Audiobooks for Everyone

Audiobooks have become very popular over the last few years. Not only do we enjoy sitting down with a good book, but we like to listen to books while we're doing other things—gardening, knitting, driving. Microsoft Edge includes a Read Aloud feature that instantly begins reading your book to you, whatever you're doing. You can switch easily from reading to listening with a simple click or tap.

When your ebook is displayed in Microsoft Edge, simply click the Settings and More tool and then click Read Aloud. Next, click the Read Aloud tool in the Read Aloud toolbar at the top of the screen. Edge immediately begins reading the text, moving the highlighted cursor as the reader reads to show you the current position.

You can change the sound or speed of the reader's voice—or even learn to add new voices to Microsoft Edge—by clicking or tapping Voice Settings in the Read Aloud toolbar.

Pick Up Where You Left Off

One of the great features of Edge is the "pick up where you left off" feature, which enables you to continue reading your ebook when you switch from your computer to tablet to phone (assuming they are all Windows devices and you've logged in with your Microsoft account). You can find a link to the place you stopped in the Windows 10 Action Center. (Swipe in from the right or click the notifications icon to see it.)

Saving Articles to Your Reading List

Chances are good that you often find articles you want to read but don't have time. Microsoft Edge includes a Reading List tool that enables you to save content for later so you can read through it when you are ready.

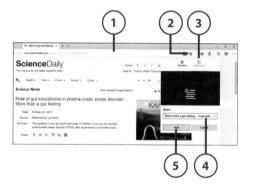

1. Display the page with the content you want to add to your Reading List.

2. Click the Hub tool.

3. Click the Reading List tool.

4. Type a new name, if you like.

5. Click Add. The article is added to your Reading List.

When You're Ready to Read

When you have a few moments and are ready to read the article you saved, click the Hub tool in the toolbar on the upper-right portion of the screen. Click Reading List, and your article will be among those listed there in the Reading List pane.

Adding Notes to Web Pages

Now you can add notes to web pages and save and share them with friends whether you're using a tablet, a phone, or a mouse and a desktop PC. When you create a note, you can save it to a OneNote notebook (which you can then share easily with others) or save it to your favorites or reading list.

1. Display the web page where you want to add the notes.

2. Click the Add Notes tool.

3. Choose the tools you want to use.

4. Write your note on the page.

5. Click or tap the Save Web Note tool.

6. The Hub opens, showing a OneNote tab.

7. Choose the notebook section where you want to save the note.

8. Click or tap Save. Microsoft Edge saves the note to your OneNote notebook.

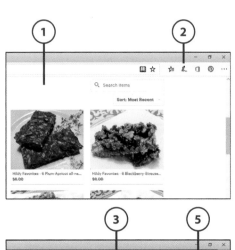

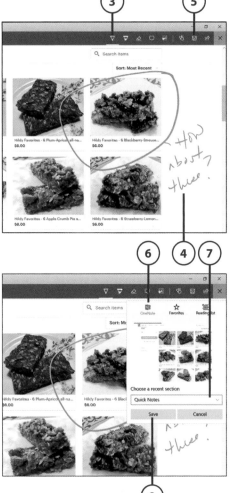

Printing Web Content

Microsoft Edge includes a new printing engine that gives you a wider range of options for the ways in which you print web content.

1. Display the page with the content you want to print.

2. Click the Settings and More tool.

3. Click Print. The title of the web page appears in the title bar of the Print window.

4. Click the Printer arrow to choose where you want to print the page.

5. Click Orientation if you want to change the printed page from portrait to landscape orientation.

6. Choose the number of copies you want to print by clicking the increase or decrease buttons or by typing in the box.

7. Choose whether you want to print all pages in the document or selected pages.

8. Click to choose the size at which you want to print the page.

9. Click to choose from among normal, narrow, moderate, or wide page margins.

10. Choose whether you want to print headers and footers on the page.

11. Click Print to print the page.

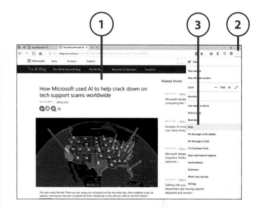

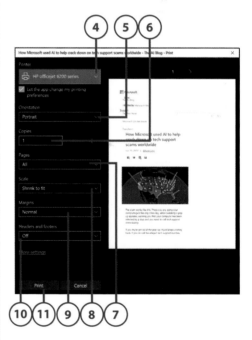

Securing Your Browsing Experience

Microsoft Edge includes security features that help Microsoft identify and safeguard against any threats before they are downloaded to your browser window. You also have a number of options for controlling the data you receive and share as part of your browsing experience.

>>>Go Further
WHAT'S ALL THE FUSS ABOUT DO NOT TRACK?

Do Not Track is a setting that tells web pages you visit that you have opted not to have your browsing habits recorded. This is a good thing for consumer privacy, but online advertisers who sell ads based on traffic statistics and user browsing data are up in arms about the possibility.

To turn on the Do Not Track feature in your version of Microsoft Edge, click Settings and More, select Settings, and click the View Advanced Settings button. Scroll down to the Privacy and Services area and drag the Send Do Not Track Requests slider to the On position. You'll have the comfort of knowing that at least your data isn't helping to sell goods to unsuspecting consumers.

Blocking Cookies

Cookies are small bits of information that websites place on your computer to store data about you and your browsing preferences. Usually cookies are harmless, but sometimes they can put your privacy at risk.

1. Click Settings and More and then choose Settings to display the Settings pane.

2. Click View Advanced Settings.

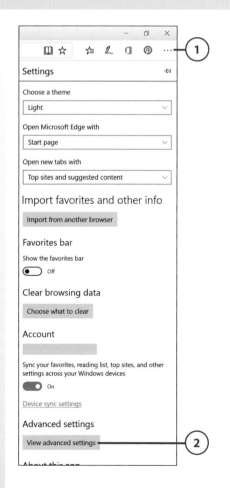

3. Scroll down to Cookies, and click the down arrow to display the list of choices: Don't Block Cookies, Block Only Third Party Cookies, and Block All Cookies.

4. Select the policy you want to use.

Cleaning Up Cookie Crumbs

It's a good idea to regularly clean off the cookies that have accumulated in your web browser, both to keep their drain on your computer's memory low and to clean out any potentially sneaky cookies that could be sending information back to the site that placed them.

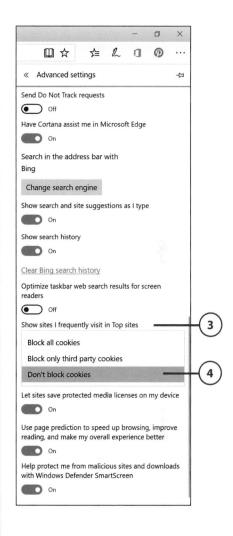

>>>*Go Further*

UNDERSTANDING COOKIE TYPES

Session cookies are cookies that are saved only while a user is on a specific site and are deleted when the user leaves that site.

Persistent cookies are cookies with a longer life span; they continue on as long as the developer specifies. In some cases, these types of cookies are helpful—they might enable you to go right to an account without having to log in—but they can also be used to accumulate data on how you browse the Web and what type of information or products you are viewing.

Third-party cookies are cookies often used by advertisers that display pop-up ads attempting to pull the user from the existing site to another site being advertised. These types of cookies can also be used for tracking purposes and could put your privacy at risk.

Clearing Browsing Data

Every so often it feels good to clear away your history, and you can do that easily in Microsoft Edge. It all starts in the Settings panel.

1. Open the Settings pane by clicking the Settings and More tool and then clicking Settings.

2. In the Clear Browsing Data area, click the Choose What to Clear button.

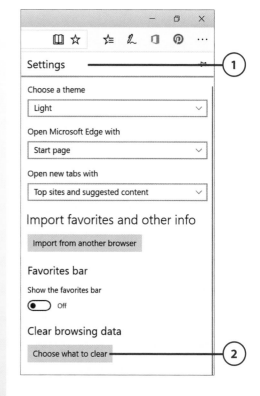

3. Microsoft Edge selects the top four items by default. Change the settings by clicking the boxes of the items you want to clear or keep.

4. Click Clear to complete the process.

5. If you want these items to be cleared every time you close your browser, move the slider to On.

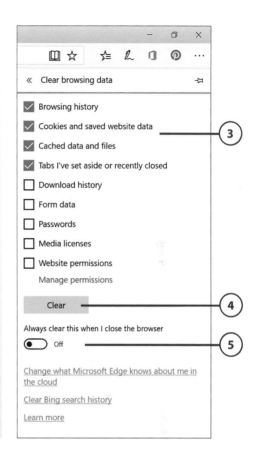

It's Not All Good

IT DOESN'T REMEMBER ME NOW

One of the downsides to clearing your history is that websites that previously seemed to remember you (for example, they knew what region you were from or what time zone you were in) have now forgotten you. If you have elected to have Microsoft Edge save your passwords and form data, however, those items will still be preserved and entered for you.

Blocking Pop-Ups

By default, Microsoft Edge turns on the pop-up blocker, so you shouldn't be getting those annoying pop-up ads that want to sell you everything from exercise equipment to vacations in the Caribbean. If you ever need to check the setting or want to turn it off for some reason (which isn't recommended), the option is in Advanced Settings.

Saving Passwords and Form Entries

We all have too many passwords these days to keep them all in our heads. Microsoft Edge can help you keep things straight, but although it does attempt to secure your data, keep in mind that anytime you store your passwords with a browser, you incur at least some security risk.

1. Display Advanced Settings by clicking Settings and More, choosing Settings, and clicking the View Advanced Settings button.

2. Scroll down to the Privacy and Services area, and slide Offer to Save Passwords to On.

3. Slide the Save Form Entries slider to the On position.

Managing Your Passwords

To manage stored passwords, display the Advanced Settings panel and scroll down to the Privacy and Services area. Click the Manage Passwords button. This displays, in the Manage Passwords pane, a list of all the sites you log in to and their corresponding passwords. If you want Microsoft Edge to forget one or more of the passwords shown on the list, point to the site and then click the Close button on the far right.

>>>Go Further
USING SMARTSCREEN

Windows Defender SmartScreen is a security tool in Microsoft Edge that helps your browser recognize and block phishing websites. Phishing is a type of predatory online practice in which perpetrators try to dupe unsuspecting web users into thinking they are visiting legitimate websites. The phishing site then gathers important information from users, including usernames, passwords, credit card numbers, and the like, which leaves the user vulnerable to identity theft and more.

SmartScreen is turned on by default in Microsoft Edge, but you can check the feature by clicking Settings and More, selecting Settings, and then clicking View Advanced Settings. You'll find the Windows Defender SmartScreen control all the way at the bottom of the list. Make sure it is set to On so that you will be alerted when you encounter any suspicious websites, and each site you visit will be checked against an ever-growing database of reported phishing sites.

The new People Hub
helps you keep favorite
contacts close.

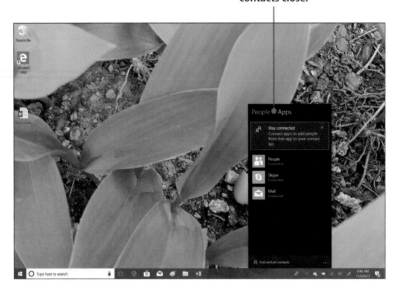

Easily see your schedule and
add to it in the Calendar app.

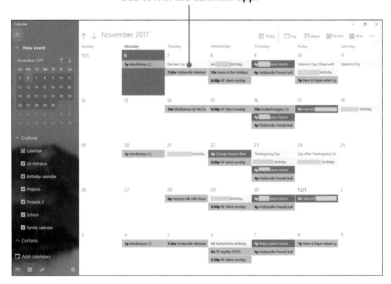

In this chapter, you learn to use Skype, the People app, and the Mail and Calendar apps to keep your connection strong with these tasks:

→ Calling and messaging with Skype
→ Using the New People Hub
→ Managing contacts with the People app
→ Staying in touch through email
→ Keeping your dates straight with the Calendar app

Staying in Touch (and in Sync) with Windows 10

So much of what we do with our computers involves communication. We call or email friends and family members, we schedule appointments and meetings, and we continually check our favorite social media sites to see what's new in the lives of those we love.

Windows 10 Fall Creators Update includes a number of tools to help us keep in touch with our favorite folks. In this chapter, you learn about the new People Hub, which helps you keep the ones you communicate with most often right at your fingertips. You're also introduced to four apps you can use to stay in touch with others. Skype is the communications app you use to call or message others in real time; you can make a web-based call (for free) or buy minutes to use with international and other toll calls. The People app serves as a hub for all your social media activities. You can bring all those updates together in one spot so you can stay on top of the latest news without opening a lot of programs. And the email and calendar apps make it simple for you to keep up with everyone at work, home, and school and keep your schedule organized and up-to-date.

Calling and Messaging with Skype

When Microsoft acquired Skype, the vision was to build a beautifully integrated communication tool that added video and voice calling, as well as instant messaging, into all sorts of Microsoft products. Skype is included as one of the apps in Windows 10 Fall Creators Update, so you never need to be out of reach of family, friends, colleagues, and clients.

Starting Skype

You launch Skype just as you would any other Windows 10 app: by choosing it from the list on your Start menu or by tapping or clicking the app tile.

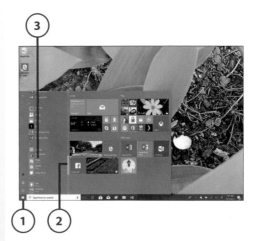

1. Click the Start button to display the Start menu.

2. Drag the scrollbar down until you see the apps that begin with the letter S.

3. Click or tap Skype.

It's Not All Good

Giving Skype Permission

Some users were having a problem with Skype during the early days of Windows 10: Skype wouldn't launch when they tapped or clicked the Skype icon. Developers found that there was a conflict over the webcam permission, and it was a simple fix. If your version of Skype isn't starting up the way it should, close the Skype app, display Settings, choose Privacy, and select Webcam (or Camera). First, make sure Let Apps Use My Camera is set to On, and then make sure that in the list of apps allowed to use your webcam, Skype's setting is set to On. Correct the setting if necessary and close Settings. Restart Skype, and hopefully everything will go smoothly.

Signing In to Skype

After you download and launch Skype, the Sign In window appears. You can sign in with your Skype name (if you have one), your Microsoft account, or even your Facebook account. If you would rather use a different Skype account than the one shown on the Sign In screen, click the Sign In with a Different Account link and enter your account information.

1. Check your sign-in account.

2. Click or tap Sign In.

3. If you want to use a different account, click the link and enter the sign-in information you want to use.

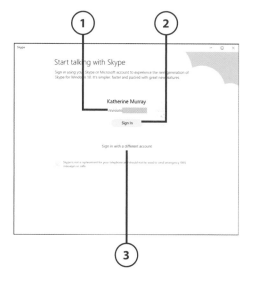

Call Everywhere, for Free

Skype Click to Call is a feature that plugs Skype into the Web so that when you see phone numbers listed online—for example, with restaurants, contacts, and so on—you see a link and a small Skype icon. This happens because you have Skype Click to Call installed. You can click the number to make the call instantly, for free. Nice.

Exploring the Skype Window

After you're signed in, the Skype window is fairly easy to navigate. You'll see a number of familiar features as you work with the tools in the program:

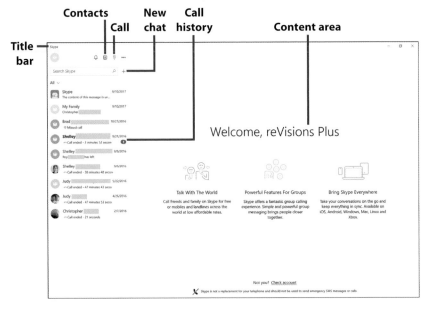

- The title bar at the top of the window shows the app name and your sign-in username, as well as the window controls on the far right.

- The Skype tools give you what you need for managing your Skype account, finding and adding to your contacts, reviewing conversations, making calls, organizing the Skype view, setting Skype options, and getting help.

- The Call History pane includes your profile information, the Search tool, and a list of recent calls.

- The Content area displays the Skype Home page at first, but when you make a call or chat with friends, your interactions happen in this area of the Skype window.

Receive Calls Anytime

Even if you've set your Skype availability to Invisible, the calls still come through in Windows 10. You get a notification about the incoming call and, if you miss it, a Skype notification icon appears on your Lock screen, letting you know how many calls you've missed.

Finding and Adding Contacts

Conversations are the focus and trade of Skype, so you can start, end, and add to conversations—which might be calls, video chats, or text messaging threads—easily. You can add contacts to your list by initiating contact with them or add them to ongoing conversations.

1. In the Skype window, click Contacts.

2. Click or tap in the Search box.

3. Type the name of the person you want to find.

4. Scroll through the results list.

5. Click the name of the person you want to add as a contact. The contact is added to the communication window.

6. Start a conversation with the new contact by sending him or her a text message.

7. Click to start a video call.

8. Click to launch a phone call by Skype.

9. If you want this contact to show up in your list of Favorites, click or tap the star to the left of the contact name.

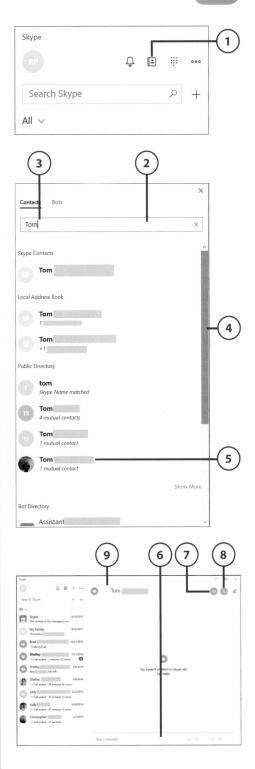

Connecting Your Address Book

You can connect your address book to Skype so the app can find all your contacts easily. Click the Contacts tool in the main Skype window, and in the list box that appears, click the Connect Address Book link. Skype asks you to enter and verify your phone number and then requests your permission to access your contacts. After you complete the process, your contacts will be available for contact through Skype.

Communicating with Skype

Communicating with others in Skype is easy. You can choose whether you want to make a video call, make an audio call, or send a text message, all with a simple click.

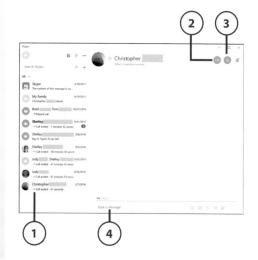

1. Click or tap the contact you want to call. The contact screen opens in the right pane.

2. Click or tap to open a video call.

3. Click or tap to begin an audio call.

4. Type to send an instant message to the contact.

How Do I Contact Thee? Let Me Count the Ways

The question of whether your contact is online when you're trying to contact her makes a difference in the number of tools you see in the contact window. If your contact is not online, you see only the green video call and audio call buttons in the upper-left corner of the screen, at the bottom of the contact's profile picture. If the contact is online, a blue button appears that enables you to add and send files, send a video message, or add participants to an active call.

Choosing Your Messaging Service

The messaging service Skype displays just above the message box varies, depending on the source of the contact you've selected. If your contact is from the list compiled in the previous Messaging app, the selection might read Via Messaging. If you click the down arrow and select SMS Mobile, Skype prompts you to buy Skype credits for sending SMS messages.

Using the New People Hub

One of the fun new features in Windows 10 Fall Creators Update is the People Hub. Developers realize that even though social media has gotten wildly popular and we keep up with the happenings of dozens (or maybe hundreds!) of people each day, we really communicate regularly each day with only a handful of friends and family members.

The People Hub is designed to bring those contacts close so you can easily check in with them throughout your normal day. Your favorite contacts are essentially "pinned" to your taskbar so they are always within easy reach.

Getting Ready to Use the People Hub

The People Hub requires a little bit of setup before it is ready to use.

1. Click or tap the People tool on the taskbar.

2. Click or tap Get Started. The People Hub shows you which apps are currently connected to the Hub.

3. Click the icon for any app you want to change or view.

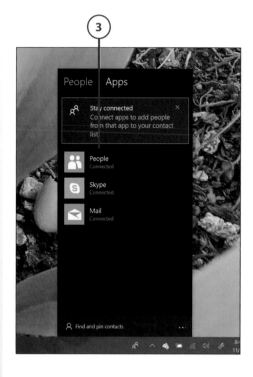

Finding People Hub Contacts

Next, you need to find and add the contacts you want to include in the People Hub.

1. Click People. The Hub offers a couple of suggestions for contacts you might want to pin to the taskbar.

2. Click the contact you want to add, and the People Hub pins the contact to the taskbar to the left of the People Hub tool.

3. If you don't see the contact you want to add, click in the Search box. A list of contacts appears.

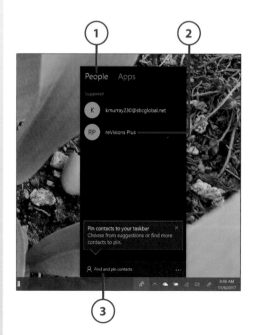

4. Type the name of the contact in the Search box.

5. Click the contact from the displayed list. The icon for the contact is added to your taskbar.

Checking In

Now that your contacts are pinned to your taskbar, you can see what's happening with them and check in through the day easily. When you get an email or a call from a pinned contact, Windows 10 lets you know right away by displaying a small number along the bottom edge of the pinned contact icon.

1. Click the contact icon when you see a notification.

2. The People Hub opens, showing the contact you selected.

3. Click the app that shows the notification icon.

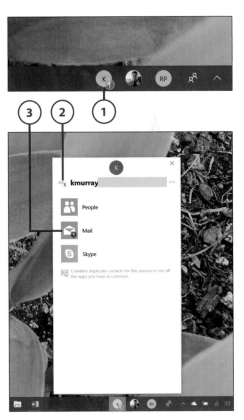

4. Click to view and reply to the message in the People Hub panel.

5. Click to open the message and review and respond in the full app.

Managing the People Hub

It's possible that over time you will want to remove someone from the People Hub and add others. You can easily remove a contact from the People Hub by unpinning that person from your taskbar. Simply right-click the pinned contact and choose Unpin from Taskbar, and the contact icon disappears (but is still available in the People Hub and in your regular contacts list).

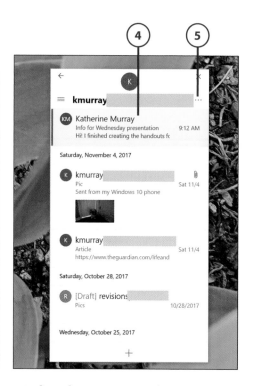

Managing Contacts with the People App

As you keep up with friends and family through email and instant messaging, do you find yourself always wondering where you saved the contact information you need? The People app in Windows 10 might be able to help by consolidating your various contacts and displaying them all in one alphabetical list, where you can find who you need easily.

Getting Started with the People App

You launch the People app from the Start menu. If you've moved your tiles around or you don't see the People app on your Start menu, you can locate the app in the All Apps list.

1. Click to display the Start menu.

2. Click or tap the People app. The People app launches.

3. If you want to import contacts from another app, click Import Contacts.

4. Click Ready to Go to start using the People app.

Using the People App

The People app window is a good example of an app that makes effective use of all available space. You can use this one window to do almost everything you need to do related to managing contacts.

1. Search for contacts by typing a name in the Search box.

2. Choose a contact by clicking a name.

3. Review contact information.

4. Edit contact info if needed.

5. Share or delete the contact if you like.

6. Add a new contact.

7. Review your most recent interactions with the selected contact.

8. Display and change settings for the People app.

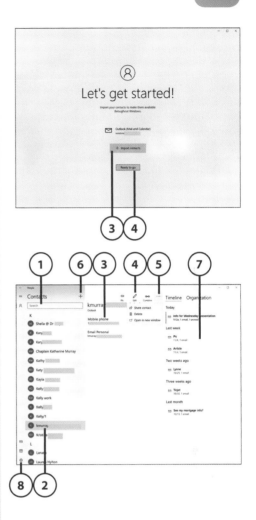

Connecting Other Contact Lists

You can connect Windows 10—and specifically, the People app—to as many mail accounts as you'd like. You set up your accounts in the Settings page of the People app. Click Settings in the lower-left corner of the People app window and click Add an Account.

Choose the account you want to connect and click Next. (You might be prompted to enter your email address and password.) Follow the prompts on-screen to give the app permission to use your information, track your location, and access the contact list. (You can always opt out, of course.) Click Done when you're finished. If you've given Windows 10 the necessary permissions, your contacts automatically show up in your People app from here on out.

Adding a New Contact

The People app provides you with a one-stop shop for all your contact needs. You can easily add, remove, edit, and delete contacts in the People app. Any contacts you add in the People app are available in your Mail app as well.

1. In the People app, click the New Contact button at the top of the pane.

2. Enter the name of the contact. If you want to add more information, such as entering the first and last name separately or providing a nickname, click the Edit tool to display a list of additional items you can add.

3. Enter the mobile phone, email address, and address information for the contact.

4. Click or tap Add Photo to display the Photos window.

5. Click or tap the photo you want to add to the contact.

6. Tap or click Save to save the new contact to your People app.

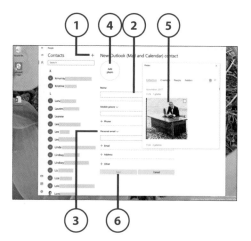

Staying in Touch Through Email

The Mail app in Windows 10 has been greatly improved. Not only is the screen clean and easy to navigate, but you can add more than one email account so all your mail comes to one central location.

The Mail app is available in the Start menu. The live tile shows you the title and intro text of your latest email message, and the number of unread messages in your Inbox is displayed on the tile. When you click or tap the app tile, the app opens on the screen, and you can click or tap the types of messages you want to see. You can view your Inbox as usual, or you can choose Social Updates to see what your friends are up to, choose Newsletters to read through your latest newsletters, or choose Flagged to see the messages you've flagged for follow-up later.

Launching Mail

You'll find the Mail app in the Start menu. You can launch the app easily by clicking or tapping the tile.

1. Click the Start button to display the Start menu.

2. Click the Mail app tile.

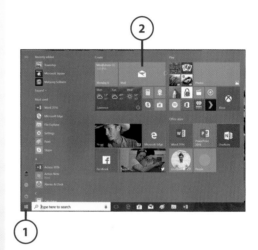

Maximize the Effect

Mail opens in a minimized window on your screen. To get the full effect of Mail (and to see the Preview pane, which shows the contents of the selected message), maximize the window by clicking the Maximize tool in the controls in the upper right.

Checking Out the Mail Window

The Mail app presents a streamlined, easy-to-navigate screen that allows you to review your mail quickly, click the message you want to read, organize your mail into folders, and respond easily to the current message.

1. Click to open a new message.

2. Click or tap a message to read it.

3. Respond to the current message.

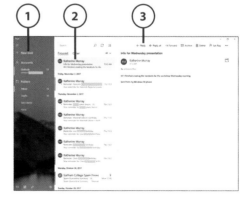

4. Delete the current message.

5. Click Focused to see email from your contacts.

6. Click Other to see general email from people who are not in your contacts list.

7. Check for new mail.

8. Display Mail settings.

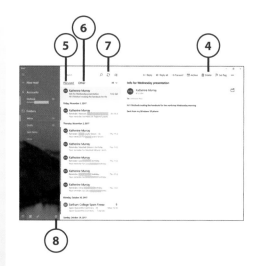

Sleek New Look

The new design for the universal Windows 10 Mail app is stream-lined and inviting. When you click the Collapse tool just beneath the app title, the left pane closes to display the Mail toolbar along the left edge of the app window.

Composing an Email Message

Creating a new message is a simple task. Here's how:

1. Display a new message by click-ing New Mail.

2. Click to choose the mail account you want to use to send the mes-sage.

3. Click or tap in the To box and begin to type the contact's name. The names of individuals in your People app appear; you can click to select the name you want to use.

4. Click in the Subject line and type a message subject.

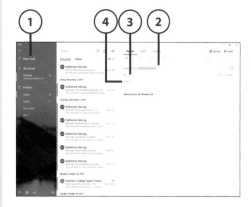

5. Click in the message area and type your message. Use the tools in the Format tab to apply the text format you want.

6. Click the Insert tab if you want to attach a file or add a table, picture, or link to the message.

7. Click the Options tab for tools to check spelling, change the language, or set the priority of the message.

8. Click Send to send the message.

9. Click Discard to delete the message without sending it.

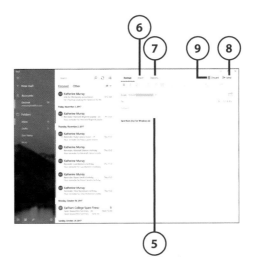

>>>Go Further

SPRUCING UP THE BACKGROUND

In Windows 10, the Mail app allows you to create a prettier background if you like. You can customize the look to give your communications a little more ambiance. Click the Settings tool and choose Personalization. In the Background section, click the Browse button and select the image you want to use. Click Open to add it to the Mail app.

Adding an Email Account

Windows 10 makes it easy to add and switch among email accounts, so you have all your email gathered in one handy place. By default, Windows 10 has likely set up the mail account you use with your Microsoft account, but you can add others as well, including Gmail, Yahoo! Mail, and more.

1. In the Mail app window, click Settings at the bottom of the left pane. The Settings pane appears along the right side of the app window.

2. Click Manage Accounts. The Settings panel appears.

3. Click Add Account.

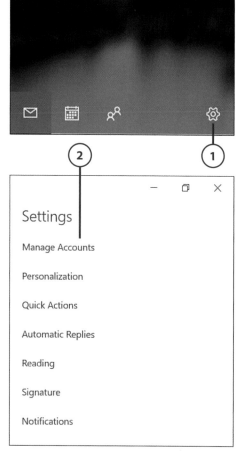

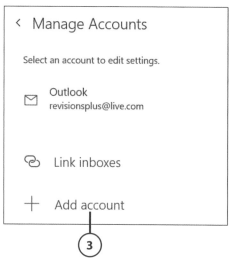

4. Click the type of account you want to add.

5. Enter the email address for the account.

6. Click Next and follow the prompts to complete the process. The Mail app adds the account to your email accounts and displays the accounts in the Accounts pane on the right side of your Mail app window.

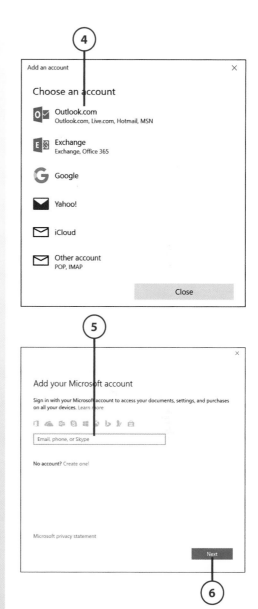

4

Add an account   ×

Choose an account

O Outlook.com
   Outlook.com, Live.com, Hotmail, MSN

E Exchange
   Exchange, Office 365

G Google

   Yahoo!

   iCloud

   Other account
   POP, IMAP

                                                    Close

5

                                                                  ×

Add your Microsoft account

Sign in with your Microsoft account to access your documents, settings, and purchases on all your devices. Learn more

Email, phone, or Skype

No account? Create one!

Microsoft privacy statement

                                                          Next

6

>>>Go Further
CHANGING ACCOUNT SETTINGS

You can tweak the settings of your email account to specify how often you want to check for new content, which types of information you want to download, and whether the account shows notifications on your Windows desktop or Lock screen. You can also remove the account if you like.

Display the Mail app window and click Settings. Choose Manage Accounts, and then click the account you want to change. You can modify the account name, let Windows know when you want to download content, and choose the items you want to sync. (You can select Email, Contacts, or Calendar.) You can change notifications by clicking the Show Email Notifications arrow and choosing whether you want to see notifications for all mail, email from favorite contacts, or never.

When you want to return to the Mail app, click elsewhere in the Mail window to clear the Settings pane.

Organizing Your Email

You might get dozens or even hundreds of messages each day. Some might be junk mail, but others you need to keep—perhaps notes about upcoming meetings, deadlines, or fun plans. You can organize your mail by filing it away in folders you create, or you can pin a message to your task list so you'll remember to follow up on it sooner rather than later.

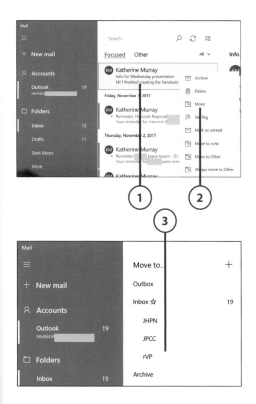

1. In the Mail app, right-click the message you want to file. A context menu appears.

2. Click Move. A list of folders appears.

3. Click the folder where you want to store the message.

Marking Mail as Junk

It's just part of emailing today—you are going to get junk mail. To get rid of the junk mail, select to move the message as outlined here and, when the Folder list appears, click Junk Email.

Keeping Your Dates Straight with the Calendar App

The Calendar app gives you access to appointments whether you're working on your desktop, tablet, or phone. Because the Calendar app offers live notifications, you can have Windows display your appointments on the Lock screen of your computer so you don't even have to log in to see what's next in your day.

Mail and Calendar, Hand in Hand

You can move from the Mail app to the Calendar app without ever returning to the Start menu. Click the Calendar tool in the bottom of the left pane of the Mail app to open the Calendar. Similarly, you can click the Mail app in the lower-left corner of the Calendar to move back to Mail.

Checking Appointments

The first place you'll see your calendar information is on the Lock screen of your computer. You'll also notice the live tile updates on the Calendar app tile on the Start screen. You can tap the Calendar app to display your calendar, which opens by default in Month view.

1. You can display the Calendar app while you're working in Mail by clicking the Calendar tool in the lower-left corner of the Mail window. (You can also get to the Calendar from the Start menu.)

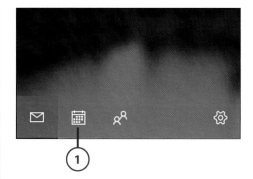

2. Review appointments in the month.

3. Click to review a specific appointment.

4. Click a different view.

5. Click the Collapse button to hide the calendar panel and get more room for calendar display.

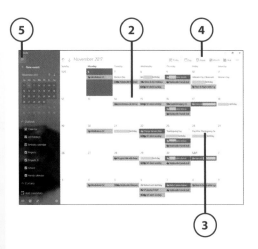

Adding a New Appointment

Creating a new appointment takes just a couple clicks and very little typing. Click the New Event tool, and then enter the information relevant to the appointment you're noting.

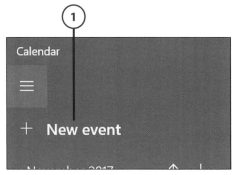

1. In the Calendar app, click the New Event tool.

2. Type a title for the event.

3. Enter the location where it will be held.

4. Enter a description describing the event.

5. Choose the date and start time for the appointment.

6. Choose the end day and time for the appointment.

7. Invite others to the event.

8. Tap or click Save and Close.

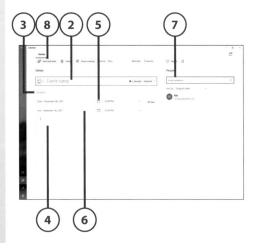

All-Day Appointments

Instead of choosing an end time, enable the All Day check box if you want to block out the entire day, or multiple days, for this appointment.

Making an Appointment Private

If you want to make sure that an appointment doesn't show up on a shared or public calendar, click the Private (lock) icon in the top right of the new event window. You'll be able to see the appointment in your calendar, but others who have permission to view your calendar will not see it.

>>>Go Further
INVITING OTHERS TO YOUR SHINDIG

While you're filling in the details for your new appointment, you can invite others to participate. In the pane on the right side of the appointment window, tap or click in the Invite Someone box, and type the email addresses of the people you'd like to invite.

After you're finished filling out the appointment form, tap Send to send the invitation to everyone involved. Each person receives an invitation with Accept, Tentative, Decline, Propose New Time, and Respond at the top so the invitee can take immediate action in response to your invitation.

Great improvements in the
Photos app make organizing and
editing images easier than ever.

Paint 3D is a fun and creative app that
makes creating 3D objects easy.

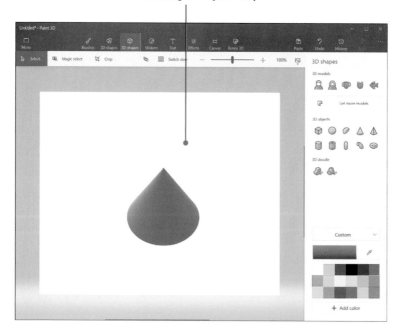

In this chapter, you learn how to work with photos, music, video, and games by learning about these tasks:

→ Viewing and organizing your photos
→ Working with creations
→ Paint 3D: Adding artistic dimensions

Bringing Out Your Inner Artist with Photos and Paint 3D

Remember the days—in the not-too-long ago past—when you took film to the drug store and then waited three days for your pictures to be developed?

Technology has made capturing, viewing, and sharing photos an instant thing, and because of that, and social media sites such as Facebook and Instagram, photographs have become a major language of connection among people all over the world. We are drawn to photos, whether they are beautiful, tragic, or interesting, and we capture and share the photos that help us communicate what's important to us.

Whether we're using our phones, tablets, or—um, cameras—taking photos is now a regular part of what we do. And the prevalence of photo-taking means that we have mountains of digital photographs to manage and organize. How will we find the one specific one we're looking for?

Windows 10 Fall Creators Update includes an enhanced Photos app that makes both organizing and fine-tuning photos simple. You can even create custom videos from the photos you've taken. What's more, the new Paint 3D app enables you to play in a multidimensional space, designing new and creative landscapes for your artistic ideas.

Viewing and Organizing Your Photos

If you've been following along and trying the various versions of Windows 10 as they become available, you have no doubt noticed that the Photos app has more than a few makeovers. In past incarnations of Photos, developers have expanded the various editing tools available. Now in the version of Photos included with Windows 10 Fall Creators Update, Microsoft has made some interesting changes that make organizing your photos easier than ever while preserving the solid editing tools. The newest version of the app also includes some new creative tools.

Starting the Photos App

It's no surprise that the Photos app is in Windows 10 in the Start menu. When you launch the app, it opens and displays the folders in which your various photos are currently stored.

1. Click the Start button to display the Start menu.

2. Click the Photos app tile.

3. Scroll down to look through your most recent photos in the displayed collection.

A Look Around the Photos App Window

The Photos app has a clean new look, and the photos are organized center stage. Across the top, the app organizes your recent photos into albums for you, so you can easily navigate through all the photo collections the app gathers from your PC, phone, tablet, and OneDrive account. Here are the tools you'll use regularly in the main window of the Photos app.

1. View your photos from all your devices, organized by date.

2. See the video albums the Photos app has put together for you (arranged by date, time, location, or subject).

3. View your photos grouped by the person central to the picture.

4. Navigate to a specific folder containing images you want to view.

5. Click to create a custom video of the photos you've taken.

6. Click to select individual photos or groups of photos.

7. Click a photo to display it and gain access to editing tools.

8. Select settings and preferences for the Photos app.

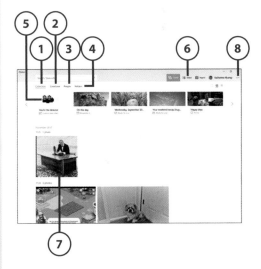

More Tools for Editing and Sharing

When you open a particular photo by double-clicking it, you'll also see a set of editing and sharing tools, which you'll learn about in the section "Editing and Enhancing Photos."

In the Windows 10 Photo app, you can choose the way in which you want to display and work with your photos. You can use collections, albums, or folders to find the images you want to use.

Collections organize your photos by date. Depending on when you took them or uploaded them, they are grouped by the date they were added.

Albums are automatically generated by the Photos app to pull together related photos—for example, one might be named something like, "Your Weekend Recap." You simply need to add them all at once to your Pictures folder, and the Photos app will make an album out of them.

The Collection view is a gathering of all your photos from a variety of places—your PC, OneDrive, your phone, and more. The Photos app displays your photos by date, with the most recently captured showing at the top. The app eliminates any duplicates, so you won't be viewing the same image more than once.

Viewing Your Photos

You can choose how you want to view and scroll through your photos by using the Collections, Creations, People, or Folders view.

1. In the Photos app, click the view you want to use.

2. Scroll through the various choices in that view.

3. Click the photo you want to view.

4. Magnify or reduce the image size by clicking the Zoom tools at the top of the photo window.

5. Browse through photos by clicking the Next or Previous buttons on the sides of the image.

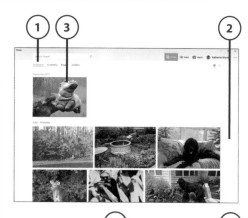

Displaying File Information

If you want to know more about a particular photo, such as when it was taken or where it was saved, click the See More tool to display the drop-down menu, and then click File Info. The Photos app shows you the name of the file, the date and time it was taken, the image resolution, the file type, and the size. You will also see where the file was originally stored. Click the Close button in the upper-right corner of the File Info panel to hide the information.

Editing and Enhancing Photos

When you're displaying an image in the Photos app, you can easily make corrections, apply filters, remove red eye, and more.

1. Display the photo you want to edit in the Photos app.

2. Click Edit & Create in the tools row above and to the right of the photo.

3. Choose Edit. A palette of editing tools appears to the right of the photo.

4. The Enhance tab provides you with a number of filters you can apply to the image. Click one to apply it.

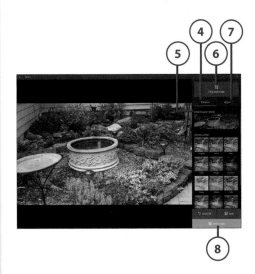

5. To have Photos auto-adjust the color, brightness, and contrast, click Enhance Your Photo.

6. Click to crop or rotate the photo.

7. Click to adjust individual levels of Light, Color, and Clarity in the image.

8. If you want to create a copy of the original picture that saves your edits, tap or click Save a Copy.

9. If you want to update the original version of the picture with your changes, click Save.

10. If you want to reverse your most recent edits, click or tap Undo All.

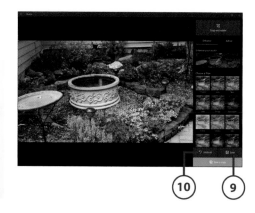

10   **9**

Importing Photos

These days we take so many photos that we need an easy way to view, edit, and share them. If you have set up your phone to work with OneDrive so you upload images you capture automatically, they're available in your Photos app without your doing anything at all (provided you use the same Microsoft account for both your OneDrive account and your Windows 10 computer or device).

If you save photos on a thumb drive or a DVD, you need to be able to tell the Photos app where to find those images so they can be imported.

1. Open the Photos app and click the Collection tab.

2. Click Import to open the sub-menu.

3. Click whether you want to import photos from a USB device or another folder. If you choose a USB device, Windows 10 looks for the device connected to your computer; if one isn't found, Windows 10 prompts you to insert it. If you choose a folder, the Open dialog box opens so you can choose the folder you want to use.

4. Navigate to the folder with the images you want to import, and click it.

5. Click Add This Folder to Pictures to tell Photos to include this folder in searches and collections.

Working with Creations

Creations are a new feature of Windows 10 Fall Creators Update. The Photos app chooses a selection of your photos (usually organized by date or person) and creates a video of images, complete with music and zoom effects. The result is quite stunning.

You can also create your own creations on the fly. The Photos app gives you the choice of creating a custom album with photos and videos you choose or editing your own video (compiled from photos you've taken).

Adding Your Own Creations

Creativity is a big theme in Windows 10 Fall Creators Update, and the Photos app gives you a number of tools and the latitude to create projects based on the photos you capture. Here's how to create your own Photos creation.

1. Open the Photos app.

2. Click or tap Create to see a list of choices.

3. Click or tap Album. The New Album window appears.

4. Scroll through the list of photos.

5. Click the photos you want to add to the album.

6. Click or tap Add. The new album is displayed so you can watch or edit your new creation.

Videos, Too

You can follow the same process to create a custom video of your favorite photos. In the Photos app window, choose Create and then select Video Project. Choose your photos and click Add, and, when you get to the editing stage, Windows 10 prompts you to add music, adjust the timing of photos, and more.

Viewing and Editing Creations

The Photos app in Windows 10 Fall Creators Update also does some creating of its own. You'll notice that the app has taken some of your photos and put them to music, animating them in a kind of video project. You can view and edit these creations to add your own creative touches.

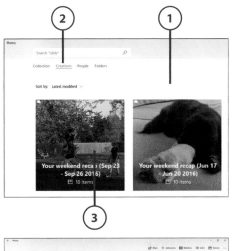

1. Display the Photos app.

2. Click Creations.

3. Click or tap the creation you want to view. The page for that project opens. The banner on the page shows a preview of the video.

4. Click Play to watch the video, complete with music.

5. Click or tap to edit the video, adding your own photos.

>>>*Go Further*

READY, SET, CAMERA

Windows 10 also includes a Camera app that you can use to grab your own still photos or videos. You'll find the Camera app on the Start menu, and when you tap or click it, after giving the app permission to use your location, you see yourself—surprise!—on the screen, with two tools to the right, offering you the option of taking snapshots or choosing video. You can also click the See More button in the top right to set an automated timer, or you can change the settings of the photo or video you're grabbing with the camera.

Paint 3D: Adding Artistic Dimension

Perhaps you've heard that 3D modeling is all the rage. From 3D printers (how is it possible that you can print a chair?) to multidimensional graphic design, looking at something in 3D gives us a more realistic sense of the object we're interacting with. Windows 10 Fall Creators Update includes several 3D modeling tools: Paint 3D, Windows Mixed Reality, and HoloLens support.

Windows Mixed Reality is a new platform in Windows 10 that enables users to see a blend of real and virtual realities. You'll get to try this out later in the chapter.

HoloLens technology is beyond the beginning level of this book (plus out of the reach of many of our technology budgets) because it requires a special VR headset. No worries, though—we can still have some fun with Paint 3D, which is included free as part of your version of Windows 10.

The Paint 3D app was originally planned as a replacement for Windows Paint, but thanks to customer feedback (and loyalty to Windows Paint), both apps now coexist in Windows 10. With Paint 3D, you can

- Create 3D landscapes and objects

- Make 2D drawings and turn them into 3D

- Add special effects and stickers

- Add ready-made 3D objects to your creations

- Tweak lighting, brightness, and more

Getting Started with Paint 3D

The Paint 3D app is in your Windows Start menu. Begin by tapping or clicking the Start button, and then scroll through the list to find the app.

1. Click or tap the Start button to display the Start menu.

2. Drag the scrollbar to display apps that begin with the letter P.

3. Click or tap the Paint 3D app. The app opens in your work area.

Displaying Tool Names

If you don't see the names of tools in the row across the top of the Paint 3D window, click the Show or Hide Names in the Menu button (it looks like three dots) in the far-right side of the tools row. The names of the tools appear beneath each tool.

Exploring the Paint 3D Window

The first time you start Paint 3D, you are greeted with a Welcome screen that offers getting started tips, ideas, and videos. You can click one of the items to see more, or click the Show Welcome Screen check box to remove the check mark so the next time Paint 3D starts, the Paint 3D screen is displayed. For now, press Esc if necessary to clear the Welcome screen.

You use the following tools in Paint 3D to create 2D, 3D, and mixed reality creations:

1. Choose the brush style, color, and thickness.

2. Create 2D shapes, lines, and curves.

3. Choose from a palette of ready-made 3D shapes, models, and doo-dles, and apply colors and textures.

4. Add stickers to your creation.

5. Insert text into your 2D or 3D design.

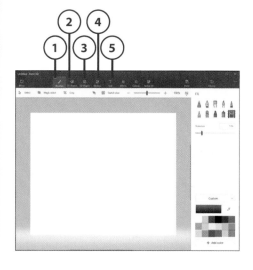

6. Apply lighting effects to the object you've created.

7. Change the size and settings of your canvas.

8. Connect to the Remix 3D community to share ideas, get new 3D objects, and more.

9. Draw or write on the canvas.

10. Choose the tools and settings you want to use. This panel displays choices related to the tools you select.

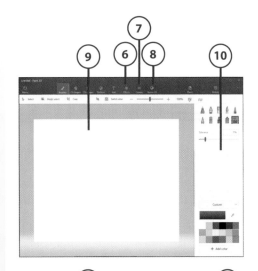

Creating with Paint 3D

There are many fun things you can do with Paint 3D, and the best way to learn is to jump in and start experimenting. Paint 3D includes many ready-made objects that you can manipulate and make part of your own drawings.

1. Using your finger or pen, click or tap the 3D tool.

2. Choose a shape from the right panel.

3. Choose a color from the color palette.

4. Drag to draw the shape on the canvas. Four tools appear around the perimeter of the shape.

5. Click a corner and resize the image by dragging.

6. Reposition the tilt of the object, forward or back.

7. Rotate the object right or left.

8. Pivot the object to get a different view.

9. Turn the object and adjust its placement in the three-dimensional space.

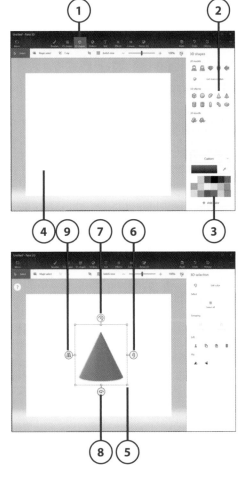

Adding Mixed Reality

Once you've created an object, you can test it out against your own reality, creating a kind of mixed experience that is fun and a little mind-bending. If your computer is equipped with a camera, Paint 3D accesses it to get a picture of the live background and displays your newly created object on it. You can move the object on the background and take a snapshot of the creation if you like.

1. Once you've created your object, click the View Model in Mixed Reality button. The object appears within the real surroundings picked up by your camera.

2. Click to position the object.

3. Rotate the object as you'd like to get the right effect.

4. Tap or click to take a snapshot of the object in the real background.

5. Click or tap Paint 3D to return to the workspace.

Saving Your Objects in Paint 3D

You can save the objects you've created by using the tools in the Paint 3D menu. You can also upload a 3D object to the Remix 3D community to share with others, invite feedback, and more.

1. When you've finished working with your object, click or tap Expand Menu.

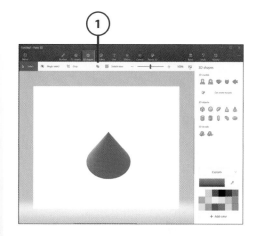

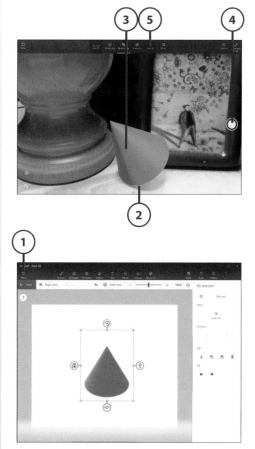

2. Click Save as Paint 3D Project. The Name Your Project box appears.

3. Type a name for the project.

4. Click or tap Save in Paint 3D.

Connecting with Remix 3D

Remix 3D is a community developed by Microsoft in which you can find a huge library of 3D objects to include in your own work. You can also upload your unique creations, talk with other 3D designers, and get tips for your work.

Display the Remix 3D library by clicking the Remix 3D tool at the right end of the tools row. A panel appears on the right side of your work area, offering a palette of ideas you can use as inspiration for your own projects. If you like, you can visit the Remix 3D community by clicking the Remix 3D menu button in the upper-left corner of the panel (it resembled three horizontal lines) and choosing Visit Remix3D.com.

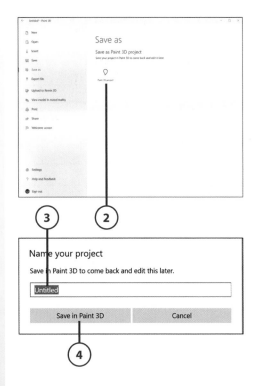

Groove Music makes it easy to find, organize, and play your favorite tunes.

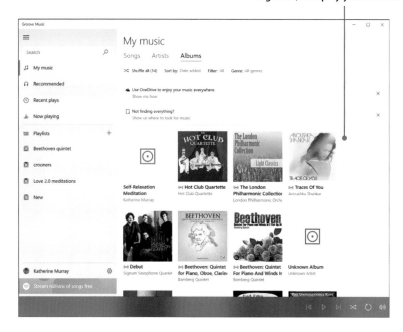

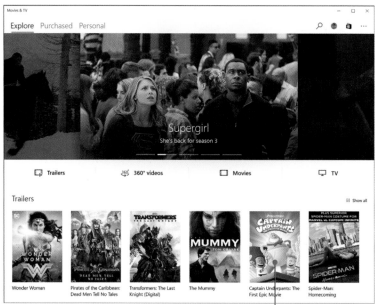

Watch your favorite shows and movies in the Movies & TV app.

In this chapter, you find out how to use Windows 10 to enjoy your favorite media—music and shows:

→ Your music, your way
→ Finding and watching your favorite shows
→ Playing and pausing shows

Getting Your Groove on with Favorite Music and Shows

From the earliest incarnations of Windows 8, great media streaming has been one of the goals of the operating system changes. Today many of us watch movies, and shows and listen to music streaming in real time. We do still buy CDs and slip DVDs in the drive once in a while, but much of the media enjoyed today is digital.

In Windows 10, you use the Groove Music app and the Movies & TV app to listen to your favorite tunes and to watch your favorite shows. Both apps are included as part of Windows 10, so they are ready to be used as soon as you're ready to be entertained.

Your Music, Your Way

In Windows 10, your media is front and center. You can get to your Groove Music app right from the Start menu, with a simple click. You can play your music in your own collection, search for the latest tunes from your favorite artists, and even purchase new music, all within the Groove Music app.

Some of the changes to the Groove Music app include a sleek new design for the Groove Music app interface, complete with a dark theme; easier access to your albums, artists, songs, and playlists; and a never-ending catalog of tunes in the Microsoft Store.

Changes for Groove

In the fall of 2017, Microsoft announced that it was doing away with the Groove Music Service, a subscription-based streaming service that enabled you to listen to albums for free if you paid a monthly fee.

To replace this streaming service, Microsoft is partnering with Spotify. çUsers who previously used the Groove Music Service will be led through the process of moving their media over to Spotify so they can continue to enjoy their favorite music without interruption. Groove Music Service was discontinued as of December 31, 2017. The Groove Music app will continue to be the standard music app in Windows 10, however, enabling you to play the songs and albums you've purchased that are stored in your Groove Music library.

Getting Started with the Groove Music App

The Groove Music app is displayed as a tile on your Start menu, and you launch it by clicking the tile.

1. Click to display the Start menu.

2. Click the Groove Music app tile. The app opens on your screen.

Playing Music

The Groove Music app usually opens to a screen displaying your Albums, although it can vary. You can click one of the albums to begin listening to your favorite tunes, or you can click another tool on the left to find a specific song, play tunes by artist, open a playlist, and more.

Learning the Groove Music App Window

The toolbar along the left side of the window gives you different ways to find and play the music you want to hear.

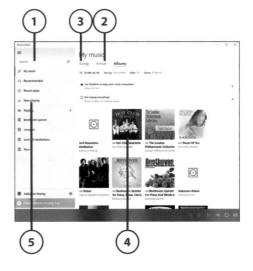

1. Click and enter the name of an artist or album you want to search for.

2. Click to display your music listed by artist.

3. Click to see a list of songs in the Groove Music app.

4. Click an album you want to play.

5. Click to display information about the album currently playing.

Expanding the Toolbar

If your toolbar is condensed, it won't look like the one shown in the figure. You can expand it by clicking the Maximize Navigation Pane button (three horizontal lines) at the top of the toolbar.

Playing an Album in Groove Music

The Groove Music app makes it easy to find and play your favorite music. In the Groove Music window, simply click the album you want to play and use the music controls in the lower-right corner of the screen to change the order, adjust the volume, and more.

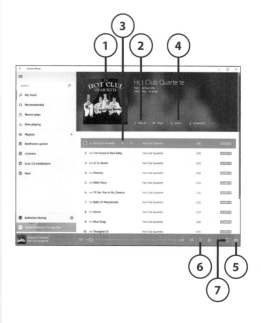

1. Click the album you want to play. The playback window appears, listing all the songs in the album.

2. Click Play All if you want to listen to the entire album.

3. If you want to play one song in the list, click it, and click the Play button that appears in the listing.

4. Click to add the selected song to a playlist.

5. Change the volume for playback.

6. Pause the playback of the current song.

7. Turn on repeat so the same song will play again.

Changing Music Settings

Like everything else in Windows 10, you can set up Groove Music to act the way you want it to. Click the Settings tool to the right of your profile picture and name in the lower-left corner of the Groove Music window.

In the Groove Music Settings window, you can click a link to move your music collection automatically to Spotify. You can also tell Windows 10 where to look for the music collection stored on your computer, choose whether you want album covers and data to be updated automatically, and determine whether songs on OneDrive will be updated as you make changes. Additionally, you can choose whether you want Groove Music to appear in light or dark mode.

Creating Playlists

Playlists are collections of favorite songs that you group in any way you like, for easy listening later. You might put together a playlist of relaxing songs, a playlist of your favorite workout tunes, or a playlist of songs you like to listen to while hiking. Creating a playlist is easy in Groove Music.

1. In the Groove Music window, click the Create New Playlist tool. The Name This Playlist window opens.

2. Type a name for the new playlist.

3. Click Create Playlist. Groove Music opens the new playlist.

4. Click Go to Albums to add music to the playlist.

5. Drag the slider to On if you want to make your playlist songs available when you're offline.

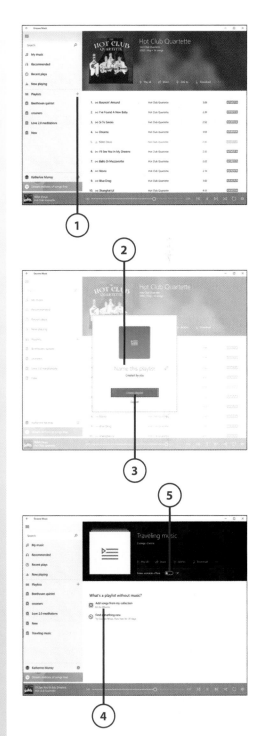

6. Click the check box to the left of the songs you want to add to the playlist.

7. Click Add To. A list of playlists you've created appears.

8. Click the name of the playlist you just created.

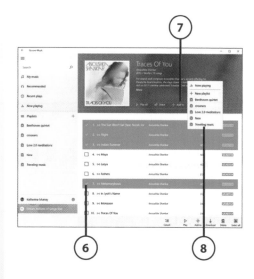

Creating a Playlist on the Fly

You can also create a new playlist on the fly by clicking a song or songs you like, clicking Add To, and choosing New Playlist. Groove Music asks you to name the playlist and then displays the selected songs in the new playlist.

Finding and Watching Your Favorite Shows

The Movies & TV app in Windows 10 is a tempting proposition, giving you access to a host of streaming movies, television shows, and other videos that you can purchase and add to your own collection. You also can learn more about your favorite movies and shows and even rent them online instantly and then stream them to your computer or to your Xbox.

It's Not All Good

RIP Media Center

Although Microsoft made Windows Media Center Edition (MCE) available as a download for those tech enthusiasts who wanted to use it with Windows 8, Microsoft has announced that in Windows 10, Media Center is officially dead and will not return. Windows Media Center arrived in 2002 and had a long run as the media hub that would enable you to enjoy movies, music, and shows to your heart's content, well ahead of the technological advances in media we see today.

With today's universe full of media-streaming and hosting apps (more than a few of which live in Xbox Live), MCE has outlived its usefulness. You had a good run, MCE. Thanks for the memories.

Launching the Movies & TV App

The Movies & TV app is available on your Start menu.

1. Click to display the Start menu.

2. Click the Movies & TV app tile. The Movies & TV app opens on your screen.

Blank Space

When the screen first opens, you may be surprised by the blankness of it. This happens because until you've purchased movies in the Movies & TV app, there's nothing to show. You can click Visit Store to begin shopping for movies, however.

Exploring the Movies & TV App Window

The Movies & TV app has been renamed from the Video app, which was available in Windows 8.1. Now the app has a whole new look and feel. The clean look and left-side toolbar give the feeling that movies and shows are center stage. Here are the main tools you'll be using with the Movies & TV app.

The tools on the Movies & TV app window make it easy for you to

1. Explore available movies and shows, display shows you've purchased, or browse videos and shows you've added to your personal collection.

2. Choose whether you want to view trailers, 360 videos, movies, or TV shows.

3. Change Movie & TV app settings.

4. Click an item to learn more and begin watching.

5. Shop for movies and TV shows in the Store.

Finding New Movies & TV Shows

The Store is available in the top-right corner of the Movies & TV app, so you can easily browse for new items to watch. If you use the Search tool to look for a show or an actor, the app displays a link offering to take you to the Store.

1. In the Movies & TV app, click Store. The Microsoft Store opens, displaying a horizontal scrolling list of recent releases.

2. Click a show you want to know more about.

3. Click to see the top movies being sold currently.

4. Click to see new TV shows that are currently popular.

5. Scroll down to see additional titles.

6. Click a show you want to know more about, and a detail screen opens for that show.

7. Click to purchase the entire season.

8. Click to purchase individual episodes.

Paying for Content

The process for paying for content can vary based on how you've set up your account. If you have a Microsoft account and have a credit card associated with it, it's a very simple process. If you don't, you'll have to jump through some hoops to set up a payment option.

Playing and Pausing Shows

Once you've found, purchased, and downloaded the shows you'd like to watch, you can make some popcorn and fire up the Movies & TV app.

1. Click or tap the Start button to display the Start menu.

2. Scroll through the apps list and click the Movies & TV app. The app window opens.

3. The Personal tab is displayed by default. This tab shows titles you have previously purchased.

4. Scroll to see additional titles.

5. Click or tap the show you want to watch.

6. If the show you've selected is a series, episodes are listed in the window. Click Play to start the show.

7. If you want to pause the show, click or tap pause. When you want to resume viewing, click Play.

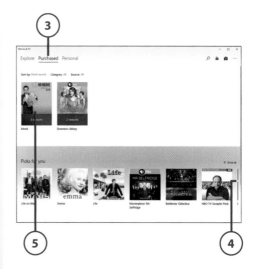

Closed captioning   Rewind   Forward   Play in Mini View

Volume

Full screen

The improved Xbox app enables you to connect with friends, join gaming clubs, play games, and more.

Seamlessly broadcast your gameplay to your own gaming channel on Mixer.com.

In this chapter, you learn how to find and play games in Windows 10 with these tasks:

→ Exploring the Xbox App
→ Playing a game with the Xbox app
→ Using the Game bar
→ Choosing game settings
→ Broadcasting as you play
→ Finding and downloading new games
→ Checking network status

Entertainment for the Gamer in You

In Windows 10 Fall Creators Update, developers recognize the importance of good gameplay for Windows 10 users. Now the Xbox app in Windows 10 has some slick new features that make gaming with friends—in the same room or across the world—easier than ever. You can record video and audio clips of your gameplay or broadcast your own gaming prowess in real time. Gone are the days of sitting alone in a room playing against a computer foe. Now gaming is a real-world community effort, organized by interest and skill, no matter what type of game you may be playing.

Exploring the Xbox App

All your gaming in Windows 10 begins with the Xbox app, which is in the Windows 10 Start menu. Once you launch the app, you'll be able to access the games you've purchased and downloaded, browse for more games, and connect with friends and the Xbox gaming community.

Starting the Xbox App and Signing In

After you launch the Xbox app from your Start menu, you are greeted with a sign-in screen that should display the Xbox gamer tag that is connected to your Microsoft account. If the gamer tag shown isn't yours (which is very possible if you live in a household with children), you can click Switch Account to choose the gamer tag that you want to use.

1. Click the Start button to open the Start menu.

2. Click the Xbox app. The app opens on your screen, sporting that sophisticated design.

3. Click Switch Accounts if you need to select a gamer tag other than the one shown.

4. Click Let's Play to open the Xbox App window.

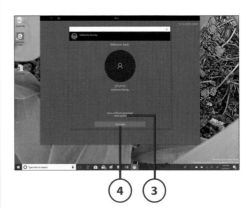

Learning the Xbox App Window

Like other universal apps in Windows 10, the Xbox app displays the toolbar down the left side of the app window. You can expand the names for the various tools by clicking the Menu tool at the top. Here are the elements you'll likely use most often in the Xbox app.

Home   **Microsoft Store**   **Friends & Clubs**

My Games
Achievements
Game DVR
Clubs
Trending

Search
Connection
Settings

- Home displays the games you've played most recently, introduces you to new games you might like, and lists an Activity Feed where you see posts, achievements, and status updates from friends.

- Friends & Clubs shows you other gamers you play with regularly (and who are connected to your Xbox Live or Xbox One account). You can also see their online status so you know whether they are available to play games.

- My Games lists the games you currently have on your PC.

- Achievements shows any badges you've earned while playing games.

- Game DVR shows screen captures or clips you've taken of games you've played on Xbox.

- Clubs enables you to find clubs of gamers who are interested in the things that interest you.

- Trending shows you what people are playing and following on Xbox Live.

- You can browse or look for specific games in the Microsoft Store.

- Search enables you to search for specific games or game content.

- Connection enables you to connect your Xbox app on your PC, tablet, or phone to your Xbox One.

- Change Settings for Notifications and Privacy.

Playing a Game with the Xbox App

Playing a game is super simple with the Xbox app. You play installed (and supported) games in your Xbox app by going to My Games and selecting the one you want to play. Microsoft also conveniently adds a link on that page that can take you to the Store to find more games to play.

1. In the Xbox app, click My Games.

2. Click the Play button for the game you want to play.

3. If you don't see a game you want to play, click Find Games in the Microsoft Store to browse games you can purchase or download for free.

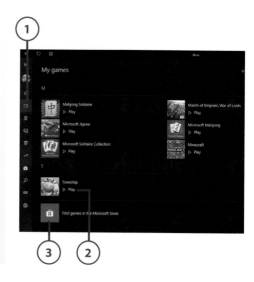

Using the Game Bar

While you're playing a game, you can display the Xbox app Game bar by pressing Windows+G. The Game bar appears in the lower part of your screen as you play.

1. Press Windows+G to display the Game bar.

2. Click or tap to return to the Xbox app.

3. Click to take a screenshot of whatever is on the screen.

4. Record a game clip of your current play.

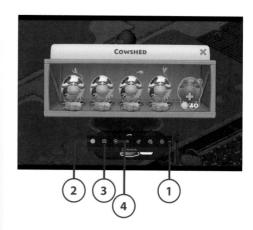

5. Start recording your gameplay.

6. Broadcast the game you're playing.

7. Turn on Game Mode.

8. Change game settings related to recording, broadcasting, and game mode.

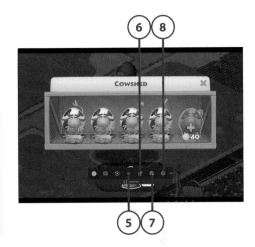

Help in Real Time

If you choose an option on the Game bar that isn't currently active, such as background recording, the Xbox app notifies you that you need to turn that setting on and instantly displays the setting you can change to make that happen. Just click the change you want and continue playing.

Using Game Mode in Windows 10

Game mode helps optimize your computer while you're playing games so you have all the processing power you need for smooth graphics, rich sound, and more. When you turn Game mode on, Windows 10 puts gaming first in terms of processing, so you get the best game quality and play you can get on your computer system.

You can turn Game mode on while you're playing a game by pressing Windows+G to display the Game bar and clicking the Game mode tool to the left of Settings on the bar. To change the settings for Game mode, click Settings in the Game bar and click the General tab. If the box next to Game mode is empty, click it to add a check mark. This turns Game mode on.

Choosing Game Settings

Windows 10 Fall Creators Update cares about gaming so much that there is now an entire category in Settings devoted to Gaming. You can set things up for gameplay all in one place or make changes while you play by using the Game bar. To view and change preferences in Settings, follow these steps.

1. Click Start to display the Start menu.

2. Click Settings.

3. Click or tap Gaming.

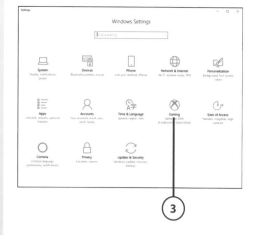

4. Make sure the Game bar slider is set to the On position.

5. Click to have the Game bar appear when you play in full-screen mode.

6. Click Game DVR to change settings related to capturing video of your games.

7. Click to change the folder where video clips, recordings, and screenshots are stored.

8. Make sure this is set to On so you can record clips in the background while you play.

9. Set the length of the video clips you want to capture.

10. Choose the maximum length of video you want to record.

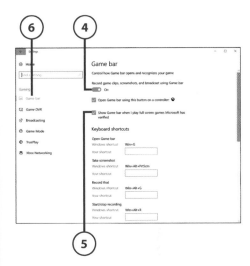

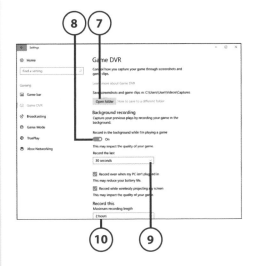

>>>Go Further
GAMEPLAY SHORTCUTS

By default, Windows 10 gives you a number of keyboard shortcuts you can use with the Game bar. If you prefer, you can assign your own keyboard shortcuts for the various tasks in the Game bar page of the Gaming Settings. These are the default shortcuts:

Open the Game bar	Windows+G
Take a screenshot	Windows+Alt+PrtScrn
Record a clip	Windows+Alt+G
Start/Stop recording	Windows+Alt+R
Show/Hide recording timer	Windows+Alt+T
Microphone on/off	Windows+Alt+M
Start/Pause broadcast	Windows+Alt+B
Show camera in broadcast	Windows+Alt+W

Play Fair with TruePlay
In Gaming Settings, Windows 10 also gives you the option of turning on a feature called TruePlay, which helps to ensure that there is no cheating going on in the games you are playing. This setting requires your permission because Windows shares the information to ensure the game is played fairly. You can turn on TruePlay by displaying Settings, choosing Gaming, clicking TruePlay, and moving the slider to the On position.

Broadcasting as You Play

If you enjoy playing games alongside others or like to share your mastery of a particular game, you will enjoy the broadcasting feature in the Xbox app. You can easily share the game you're playing on your own channel on Xbox Live. Windows 10 makes all the necessary connections for you and makes the process simple.

1. Launch the game you want to play in the Xbox app.

2. Press Windows+G to display the Game bar.

3. Choose whether you want your video and audio to be broadcast along with the gameplay.

4. Choose where you want your video image to be displayed.

5. Click or tap Start Broadcast to begin broadcasting. A small broadcast window appears in your game window.

6. This number shows you how many people are watching your broadcast.

7. Click to turn on your microphone.

8. Click to turn on your video camera.

9. Click to pause the broadcast.

10. Click to stop broadcasting.

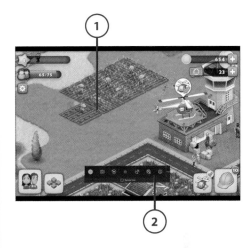

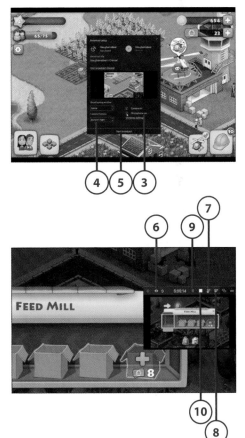

>>>*Go Further*
MIXER.COM: BROADCASTING WITH FRIENDS

When you click Broadcast and begin streaming your live game session for others to see and respond to, you are using a Microsoft service called Mixer (formerly called Beam), which enables live streaming in an online format. Windows 10 Fall Creators Update includes improvements to Mixer, so now you can switch easily to broadcasting within an active game. Not only can you get into a game stream more quickly, but Game mode gives you a boost for your computer's processing that makes broadcasting smoother and more seamless than ever.

Using Mixer, you can also view game broadcasting in clubs organized around your favorite gaming interests. Users can earn points, called *sparks*, for participating in broadcasts, and the sparks can be spent on different features in the Mixer service. As a broadcaster, you get to see who is following you and even chat with followers as you play. All of these improvements bring you one step closer to a fully integrated community gaming experience, and it's all free as part of Windows 10.

Finding and Downloading New Games

A big part of the fun of the Xbox app is that the number of games you can find and try is virtually unlimited, and more games are being added every day.

There are two different ways to access the Microsoft Store in the Xbox app. You can click My Games and choose Find Games in the Microsoft Store, or you can click the Microsoft Store icon in the toolbar on the left side of the app window.

Microsoft Store

Find games

The Microsoft Store opens, and the Games category is already selected. You can find games a number of different ways.

1. Click a featured game to learn more about it and purchase it if you like.

2. Choose a game category to see different types of games.

3. Search for games by name.

4. Scroll down to see additional game categories, including New PC Games, Best Selling Games, Top Free Games, and Best Rated Games.

5. Click a game to find out more about it.

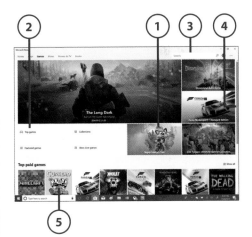

6. Read the description of the game.

7. Click to read reviews by other users.

8. Browse through screenshots of the game.

9. Click the Buy button to purchase and download the game. If the game you are viewing is free, the button is labeled Get instead of Buy. If you are purchasing the game, the Microsoft Store prompts you for payment. If the game is free, the download begins. When the game finishes downloading to your computer, Windows 10 notifies you and gives you the option of launching the game or pinning it to the Start menu.

Easy-to-Find Installs

Windows 10 also displays any new games or apps you've downloaded at the top of the Windows Start menu, in the Recently Added category.

Checking Network Status

Another new feature in Windows 10 Fall Creators Update enables you to do a network connectivity check for those times when games seem to be lagging and not working as they should. The setting is in the Gaming Settings window.

1. Choose the Gaming category in the Settings window.

2. Click or tap Xbox Networking. Windows 10 does a quick network connectivity check to see whether services are working properly and what the processing speed of your network is currently.

3. Review the network settings.

4. If you want Windows 10 to fix any network connection problems, click Fix It.

5. Click Check Again to test the network response again.

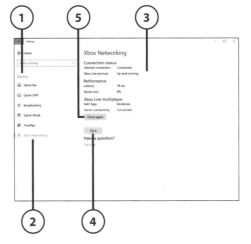

**Back up your important files
and folders automatically.**

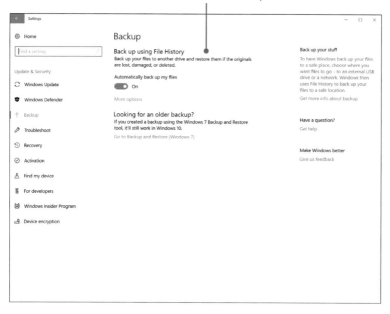

**Fix hardware or software issues
with troubleshooters.**

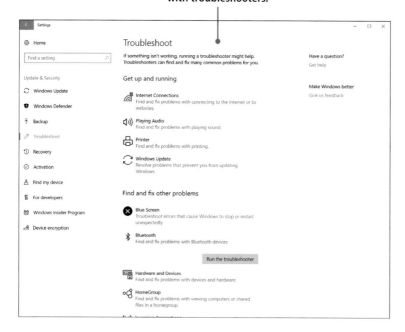

In this chapter, you learn how to care for your PC and solve problems when they arise by learning about these tasks:

→ Checking for Windows updates
→ Backing up and restoring your files
→ Troubleshooting your computer
→ Optimizing your computer
→ Encrypting your device

14

Caring for Your Computer and Updating Windows

Much of what you need to safeguard your Windows 10 computer or device happens behind the scenes in Windows 10 Fall Creators Update. Microsoft regularly updates the software, which helps ensure that you have the latest bug fixes, the most recent security patches, and other healthy tweaks that can help protect your computer and prevent crashes and security risks.

Windows 10 Fall Creators Update also adds some new features that enable you to do some of the fixing yourself. The new Troubleshoot tool offers a slate of 19 ready-to-use tools that help you sleuth out any problems you're having, whether they are hardware or software related. And although device encryption is turned on by default, you can tweak the settings or even disable the feature (although your device is safer with encryption on).

This chapter walks you through the Windows 10 tools you'll use to make sure your computer is healthy, happy, and productive.

Checking for Windows Updates

With the last big update of Windows 10, developers decided to make updating the software a "have to" instead of a "want to." They did this to ensure that all users got the security and functional patches they need to make sure the operating system is working at its optimal level. But not all people were thrilled with that—by and large, we like to make those kinds of choices ourselves.

Windows 10 Fall Creators Update does give you several options about how and when the updates are delivered, however. You can choose whether you want Windows to automatically download updates as soon as they become available; you can have Windows notify you before your system is restarted; and you can temporarily pause updates and delay them for up to seven days.

Checking for Updates

The Windows Update window lets you know when the operating system last checked for updates and gives you the option of checking again yourself. You can also set advanced update options from the Windows Update screen.

1. Display the Start menu.

2. Choose Settings.

3. Click or tap Update & Security.

4. Click the Check for Updates button. Windows Update displays a "Checking for updates" message while the operating system checks for any program changes.

5. Windows Update begins to look for available updates. If the tool finds program updates that can be downloaded, it provides information about the update and begins the download process.

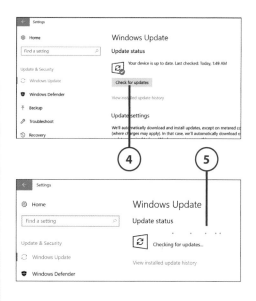

Setting Advanced Update Options

Even though you can't completely opt out of Windows updates, you can make some choices that enable you to manage your update experience. You can change when the updates are installed on your computer, and you can delay updates for a period of time.

1. Display the Windows Update screen as described in the previous task.

2. Click to specify the hours during which you don't want updates to restart your computer.

3. Click to indicate an assigned restart time (for example, 3:00 a.m.) when the restart won't affect your work.

4. Click Advanced Options.

5. If you want to pause upgrades so that the updates are postponed for a period of seven days, slide the setting to On.

6. Click to allow Windows 10 to update other Microsoft products (such as Windows Defender) along with Windows 10 updates.

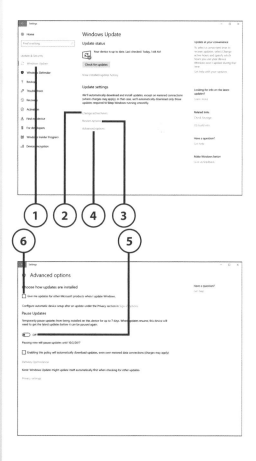

Backing Up and Restoring Your Files

Hopefully, you are already saving copies of important files and folders—
perhaps you're saving them to your OneDrive account or backing them up
on a flash drive. Making regular backups of your files helps you feel secure
knowing that your files are protected and that you have an extra copy, just in
case something happens. You can make these simple file backups yourself by
using File Explorer to copy the files to the folder or device where you want to
store the backup files.

Windows also provides a backup utility you can use to back up everything on
your hard disk. You should do this larger backup regularly—perhaps once a
week or so. This ensures that your files have been saved so that if something
unexpected happens to your computer—for example, you wind up with a
virus that damages important files—you can restore the files from your backup and go on as usual.

To get started using the Backup tool, you need to set up the utility to run the
way you want it to. This tells Windows where you want to save the backup
files and when you want to do the backup. You can change those settings at
any time, but Windows takes care of the backup automatically from here on
out on the day and time you specify.

Backing Up Your Files with File History

To back up your data, follow these steps:

1. Display the Update & Security screen in the Settings window.

2. Click Backup.

3. Click Add a Drive. Windows scans your system to find a drive where the backup can be stored.

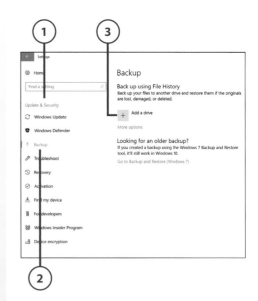

4.   Click the drive you want to use as a backup drive.

Don't Forget

If you use an external storage device connected to your PC, make sure it's plugged into your computer and has power.

5.   Windows shows the Automatically Back Up My Files control set to the On position. If you later want to suspend backups, you can drag the slider to Off.

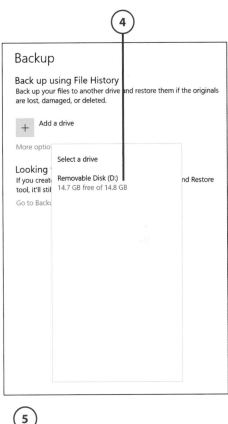

>>>Go Further
CHOOSING WHAT TO BACK UP

You can tell Windows 10 how often you want to save files and how long you want to keep file versions by clicking More Options just beneath the Automatically Back Up My Files control.

You can choose to save files as often as every 10 minutes or as infrequently as once a day. And you can choose to keep files forever (which is the default) or choose from 1 month to 2 years—or until the space is needed, whichever comes first. Finally, on the More Options screen, you can review all the folders that are included in the backup, click each one you don't want to include, and then click the Remove button that appears.

Restoring Files

You might never use the files you backed up, but it can be reassuring to have them in case you need them. If you do need them, the tool for restoring your files is in the same place you discovered the Backup tool.

1. In the Update & Security screen in Settings, choose Backup.

2. Click More Options.

3. Scroll to the bottom of the Backup Options screen.

4. Click Restore Files from a Current Backup. The Home–File History window appears.

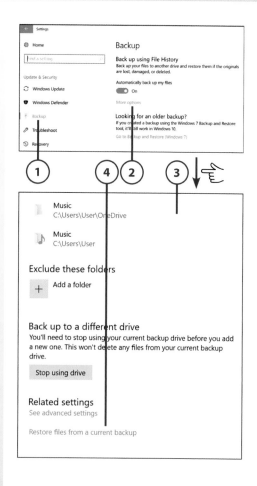

5. Click the folders you want to restore.

6. Click the Restore to Original Location button, and Windows 10 restores the backed up files for you.

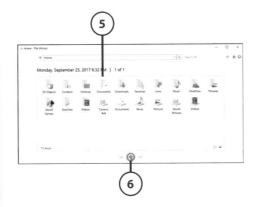

Merging or Skipping Folders

If you have an existing folder with the same name as the folder you're restoring, Windows asks you whether you want to merge the folder with the existing one or skip it. Click your choice, and the files are restored.

>>>Go Further

SAVING THE DAY WITH WINDOWS RECOVERY ENVIRONMENT

Several versions of Windows ago, Microsoft began including the Windows Recovery Environment with the operating system as a set of tools that help users recover from a variety of problems that can cause Windows to fail to start up properly. In Windows 10, this feature is very good at realizing when your computer is having troubles—when it can't boot properly or repeatedly crashes, for example—and launching the Windows Recovery Environment. This screen asks you to select between See Advanced Repair Options and Restart My PC.

Restarting your PC allows it to continue operating normally. Sometimes a good restart is all Windows really needs. Clicking See Advanced Repair Options gives you access to a set of recovery tools designed to help Windows assess and correct whatever went wrong. These tools can, among other things, restore your Windows installation to an "out of the box" state—as if it were installed for the first time.

Troubleshooting Your Computer

In Windows 10 Fall Creators Update, a new Troubleshoot category in Update & Security enables you to sleuth out problems you may be having with Windows 10. Nineteen different troubleshooters are available to help you fix everything from audio that won't play to Bluetooth troubles to issues with Windows apps.

Launching a Troubleshooter

In earlier versions of Windows, troubleshooters were around, but they were scattered throughout the operating system and not located in one handy place that was easy to find. Now Windows 10 Fall Creators Update takes the guesswork out of troubleshooters.

1. In the Update & Security screen, click Troubleshoot.

2. Scroll through the list of troubleshooters to find the one you need.

3. Click or tap the troubleshooter to select it.

4. Click Run the Troubleshooter. The troubleshooter runs a set of diagnostics and then displays a results page.

5. Click to see the details of the troubleshooting process.

6. Click to close the troubleshooter.

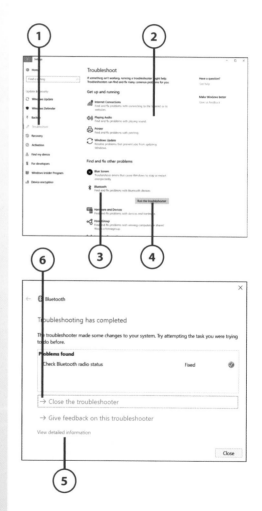

Optimizing Your Computer

In addition to regular updates and backups, you can help Windows work efficiently by optimizing the way files are stored on your computer. As part of the normal use of your computer, file bits get scattered around the hard drive. When you look at the folders in File Explorer, everything looks nice and neat, with folders and files in nice little columns. But the way your computer is actually storing the data behind the scenes isn't quite that linear. Your computer knows where everything is, thanks to the way it indexes information, but over time, bits and pieces of files can be saved in various places all over the drive. This kind of fragmentation can slow down the time it takes your computer to process regular tasks—hence the need for a tool that defragments the data your computer stores.

You can use the settings in the Optimize Drives dialog box to clean up your hard drive by consolidating those bits of files and putting them back together in one place. This can help your computer run faster and better, which is a good thing.

Optimizing Your Hard Disk

Although it runs automatically by default, running the Optimize utility fairly regularly—such as once every month or two—helps ensure that you're making the most of the available storage space on your hard drive.

1. In the Search box on the taskbar, type **optimize**.

2. Tap or click Defragment and Optimize Drives.

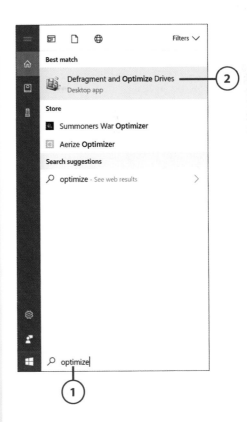

3. In the Optimize Drives dialog box, click Analyze to do a check on the selected drive to see whether optimizing it will save you any space.

4. Click Optimize to defragment the selected disk.

5. After the process is finished, click Close.

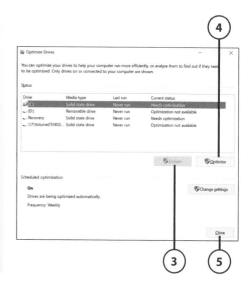

>>>Go Further

SCHEDULING REGULAR DEFRAGMENTING

You can put your PC on a steady defrag diet by having the system automatically defragment your hard drive at a specific time of the week or month. Click Change Settings in the Optimize Drives dialog box. In the Optimize Drives: Optimization Schedule dialog box, click the Run on a Schedule check box and click the Frequency you want: Daily, Weekly, or Monthly.

You can also click or tap the Choose button to select the drives you want to optimize following this schedule. Click OK to save your settings, and Disk Defragmenter will run automatically as you specified to keep your files as compact as possible.

Note that a particular type of hard drive, called an SSD, has much different rules for how it manages data (to avoid wearing it out). Windows 10 recognizes which type of drive you have and adapts accordingly.

Encrypting Your Device

Encryption is a file protection protocol that secures your files so that others can't get into them without authorization. By default, device encryption is turned on in Windows 10 Fall Creators Update. You can change that setting if you like (although for the best security, that's not recommended).

What Is BitLocker?

Windows 10 uses an encryption tool known as BitLocker to securely encrypt the files on your device. You can learn more about BitLocker at https://www.pcworld.com/article/2308725/encryption/a-beginners-guide-to-bitlocker-windows-built-in-encryption-tool.html.

Changing Encryption Settings

You can change your encryption settings—turning encryption off if you choose–by making a change in Update & Security settings.

1. Display the Update & Security window in Settings.

2. Click Device Encryption.

3. Click Turn Off. Windows 10 prompts you to confirm that you want to disable encryption.

4. Click Turn Off if you are sure you want to turn off encryption.

5. Click Cancel to leave encryption in place.

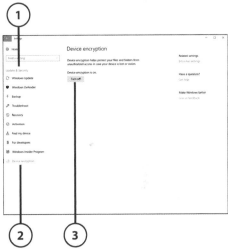

Learn More About Encryption

You can find out more about Microsoft's approach to device encryption in Windows 10 Fall Creators Update by reading "Overview of BitLocker Device Encryption in Windows 10," which is available online at https://docs.microsoft.com/en-us/windows/device-security/bitlocker/bitlocker-device-encryption-overview-windows-10.

Index

B

C

F

P

Register Your Product at informit.com/register

Access additional benefits and **save 35%** on your next purchase

- Automatically receive a coupon for 35% off your next purchase, valid for 30 days. Look for your code in your InformIT cart or the Manage Codes section of your account page.

- Download available product updates.

- Access bonus material if available.*

- Check the box to hear from us and receive exclusive offers on new editions and related products.

Registration benefits vary by product. Benefits will be listed on your account page under Registered Products.

InformIT.com—The Trusted Technology Learning Source

InformIT is the online home of information technology brands at Pearson, the world's foremost education company. At InformIT.com, you can:

- Shop our books, eBooks, software, and video training
- Take advantage of our special offers and promotions
- Sign up to receive special offers and monthly newsletter
- Access thousands of free chapters and video lessons

Connect with InformIT—Visit informit.com/community

the trusted technology learning source

Addison-Wesley·Adobe Press·Cisco Press·Microsoft Press·Pearson IT Certification·Prentice Hall·Que·Sams·Peachpit Press

 Pearson